The Essence of Time

Old Testament Survey

by

FRANKIE LUPER

Second Edition

A
COTTAGE CAFE PRESS PUBLICATION
Rockvale, Tennessee

2013

The Essence of Time

Old Testament Survey

If you can tell time, you can learn the Old Testament

Copyright 2013 by
COTTAGE CAFE PRESS

ISBN-13:
978-0988859890 (Cottage Cafe Press)
ISBN-10:
0988859890

Printed in the United States of America

ALL RIGHTS RESERVED
No part of this publication may be reproduced, stored in a retrieval system, or transmitted in any form by any means – electronic, mechanical, photocopying, recording or otherwise – without prior written consent.

Scripture quotations, unless otherwise noted, are from the King James Version or American Revised Standard Version of 1901. Used by permission.

For information contact:
Cottage Cafe Press, Rockvale, Tennessee
info@cottagecafepress.com

Dedication

This book is dedicated first to all my family. To the memory of our little boy, Donald Ray Luper, who passed from this life July 10, 1947 at the age of five. We are thankful to God because of Donnie we are a Christian family, Romans 8:28.

To my husband, Archie, whose love, encouragement and patience gave me the inspiration and motivation I needed to fulfill the admonition of the Apostle Paul when he said to "Study," II Timothy 2:15.

To our precious children, Denese and Archie, Jr., who have made my life "a little bit of heaven on earth."

To the sweetest and most precious mother in all the world, my mother, Ella Hilty.

Then to Delores Jones whose faithfulness, dedication and love for our family gave me the time and incentive I needed to devote to this work.

To Dee Hathway and Florence Warwar, two of my dearest and most precious friends who provided the encouragement, love and inspiration that I will treasure forever.

To June Foster, truly one of God's most talented and gifted women in the Church, who devoted endless hours in reading and correcting my manuscript.

Finally, to J.M. Powell and all the ladies of the Blue Ridge Encampment in Black Mountain, North Carolina. To Brother Powell for his confidence in giving me my first major teaching assignment. For the ladies of Wonderful Blue Ridge for their love and encouragement when I needed it most. To them and Brother Powell I will be forever grateful.

FRANKIE LUPER

Special thanks to Denese Rhea (Luper) Day, Kenny Luper, Florence Warwar, Dee Hathway, Josh Luper, Nick Luper, Kathy & Archie Luper, Jr. and Teah McWhorter with Chula Vista Books in Pell City, Alabama for their encouragement and assistance in re-publishing this study.

COTTAGE CAFE PRESS

Contents

				Page
I		INTRODUCTION		1
II		THE ESSENCE OF TIME CLOCKS		7
		The Periods, Books, V.I.P.'s and Bible Lands		
III	1 o'clock	Antediluvian	Genesis 1-7	21
IV	2 o'clock	Postdiluvian	Genesis 8-11	29
V	3 o'clock	Patriarchal	Genesis 12-50	37
VI	4 o'clock	Egyptian Bondage - Exodus	Exodus 1-12	47
			Exodus 13-40	
			Leviticus	
VII	5 o'clock	Wilderness Wanderings	Numbers	57
			Deuteronomy	
VIII	6 o'clock	Conquest	Joshua	69
IX	7 o'clock	Judges	Judges	79
X	7:30 o'clock	Ruth	Ruth	87
XI	8 o'clock	United Kingdom	1-2 Samuel	91
			1 Kings 1-11	
XII	9 o'clock	Divided Kingdom	1 Kings 12-22	111
			2 Kings 1-17	
XIII	10 o'clock	Judah Alone	2 Kings 18-23	125
XIV	11 o'clock	Captivity	2 Kings 24-25	131
XV	12 o'clock	Restoration	Ezra – Esther	137
			1-2 Chronicles	

Foreword

In the words of Brother Franklin Camp, preacher for the Shades Mountain congregation in Birmingham, Alabama, "The Bible is one book with 66 chapters."

The more I study, the more I can see that this is the most basic yet most important concept for the student of the Bible. It is most unfortunate that in the effort to lay aside the Law of Moses and adhere only to the law of Christ, some, in times past, simply shelved the Old Testament once and for all.

Yet, the understanding of the New Testament depends upon a good knowledge of the Old Testament. The New Testament is set against the background of the Old Testament. The writers of some of the New Testament books take for granted the reader's knowledge of the teachings of the Old Testament. And when the understanding of the Old Testament is not taken for granted, for the subject to be discussed, the writer lays the groundwork from the Old Testament just prior to the discussion. This just happens over and over again in the reading of the New Testament.

This study of the Old Testament came from my struggle to know and understand the New Testament. I could see that I was having to stop constantly and go back and try to find the background study for many portions of some books and all of other books. So I decided I needed a good working **knowledge** of the Old Testament, so I could at least know which book to go to for certain information.

Brother Camp says something else that really motivates me to a more in-depth study of the whole Bible. He says, **"The best commentary on the Bible is the Bible itself. There is no subject in the Bible that cannot be explained by the Bible."**

All things pertaining to living this life in preparation for that future life with God and Christ are explained fully and completely and it behooves us all to **study** and search the scriptures that we might know what the will of God is for us. Read 2 Peter 1:2-3; 2 Timothy 3:16-17; 2:15; in that order: then read the alternative in Hosea 4:6.

It is my prayer, then, that you join me in that **quest** to know God and to know Christ from the study of the Word of God in the whole Bible.

In Christian love,

FRANKIE LUPER

I. INTRODUCTION

The "Essence" of Time

"God planned the redemption of man before the world began."
Titus 1:22; 2 Timothy 1:9

This plan is revealed to us through the inspired Word of God, the Bible. We today are the most fortunate of all men through the ages, in that we can look in retrospect at the gradual unfolding of God's plan to redeem man back to Himself. In the Old Testament there were great men, chosen of God, who yearned to see the **fulfillment** of all they taught and wrote about Christ and His church. Isaiah wrote in Isaiah 64:4, **"For since the beginning of the world men have not heard, nor perceived by the ear, neither hath the eye seen, a God, beside thee, what he hath prepared for him that waiteth for him."** Paul quotes Isaiah in I Corinthians 2:9 in this way, "Eye hath not seen, nor ear heard, neither hath entered into the heart of man, the things which God hath prepared for them that love him." Then in verse 10 Paul says, **"But God hath revealed them unto us by his Spirit: for the Spirit searcheth all things, yea, the deep things of God."** Of course we know that Paul was speaking of the Gospel. So it was Christ and the church that Isaiah looked forward to. The **shadow** of Christ and the church is such a vital part of the Old Testament, and it should be studied as a foundation for all that the New Testament teaches.

Let's see what importance Jesus Himself places on the Old Testament scriptures. Considering first that where you find the word **scripture** or **scriptures** in the New Testament it means Old Testament, the only written word at the time the New Testament was being written.

Jesus said to the Jews in Jerusalem, **"Search the scriptures; for in them ye think ye have eternal life: and they are they which testify of me. And ye will not come to me, that ye might have life."**

John 5:39-40

Again, to the two disciples on the way to Emmaus, Jesus said, **"O fools, and slow of heart to believe all that the prophets have spoken: Ought not Christ to have suffered these things, and to enter his glory? And beginning at Moses and all the prophets, he expounded unto them in all the scriptures the things concerning himself."** Luke 24:25-27.

Then Stephen, in Acts 7, begins with Abraham and gives an entire narration on the Old Testament for his defense against the charge of blasphemy.

Of Apollos, it is said, in Acts 18:28, **"For he mightily convinced the Jews, and that publicly, showing by the scriptures that Jesus was Christ."**

Paul wrote, in Romans 15:4, **"For whatsoever things were written aforetime were written for our learning, that we through patience and comfort of the scriptures might have hope."**

Paul, in his sermon at Antioch of Pisidia, Acts 13:16-23, begins at the Egyptian Bondage, then to the nation of Israel being established and cared for by God through the wanderings, the conquest of Canaan, the period of the Judges, right up to the United Kingdom and David, to show that His purpose was always to bring a Saviour into the world and that that Saviour was Jesus.

Then Paul told Timothy, in 2 Timothy 3:15-17, **"And that from a child thou hast known the holy scriptures, which are able to make thee wise unto salvation through faith which is in Christ Jesus. All scripture is given by inspiration of God, and is profitable for doctrine, for reproof, for correction, for instruction in righteousness: that the man of God may be perfect, thoroughly furnished unto all good works."**

Of course we could quote many other passages of the New Testament testifying to the importance of a knowledge of the Old Testament, but these are sufficient to generate a desire to know all of God's plan in all of the scriptures.

The plan of God is revealed in a very orderly, progressive manner. Christianity is established historically. All other religions are conceived of and established in the lifetime of one man.

Let us consider the history of the Old Testament as the very essence of time, because it is so essential to our **understanding** the New Testament. We have far too long neglected the in-depth study of this most vital part of God's word.

To better understand the Old Testament it should be studied as a whole. **This study will emphasize the value of always knowing where a book, a period, a person or a Bible land appears in the overall scheme of things.** Each book should be studied with respect to where it appears in the whole Bible. In this way, only, can we correctly arrange God's redemptive plan for man.

"If you can tell time, you can learn the Old Testament."

Memory by association has long been established as the most natural way of teaching and learning. The Master Teacher, Jesus, used this method when He taught in **parables**. He chose those things which were readily understood by those who heard Him, with which to associate His spiritual lessons. **In this study of the Old Testament we are going to use this same method of learning, and we are also going to use something readily understood by all, the face of the clock.**

In the history of God's dealing with the children of Israel, there are 12 very natural divisions. **These 12 divisions fit readily on the face of the clock.** Thus, from the very beginning we can see the Old Testament as a whole. The additional clocks are only phases of the first clock. Each time we go around the clock, we simply are adding further information. It is imperative that we learn the Old Testament in an orderly fashion, with everyone and everything in its proper place. In this way, only, is the plan of God to redeem man back to Himself clearly understood. The **fulfillment** of the Old Testament is in Christ and His Church. By the time we finish with this study of the Old Testament, we trust we will be able to better understand the Kingdom with its intended purpose. This is the sole purpose of this study; the sole purpose for keeping the Old Testament a living part of God's word.

The most important thing to know about the use of these clocks is to thoroughly learn each clock before going to the next one. The in-depth study of each time **period** should be undertaken only when it is understood where each period fits into the Old Testament as a whole.

Also, this is not necessarily a book to be read from front to back. It is for study and the different sections would be used as you would refer to a **period** on the clock. Therefore, you will find yourself working back and forth, from one section to another. If you are studying the Old Testament in a class or if you are just reading a part of it, open the workbook and make your **notes** in the correct period, making sure to consider where the study is in the whole of the Old Testament.

If you will use this study in this manner, I am certain you will come to appreciate it as much as I have. **The clock is the most natural time line you could use for the study of the history of the Old Testament.**

My experience with the study of the Old Testament has taught me that it needs to be cut into **digestible** portions. And one of the best places to start doing this is in the categories of the books. The following diagram has worked for me.

Bible	
Old Testament	New Testament

Dispensations-Ages		
Patriarchal	Mosaical	Christian

Books of the Bible		
Genesis	Exodus to Nehemiah	Acts 2 to end of time

Categories of the books of the Old Testament:

1. Law
2. History
3. Poetry
4. Major Prophets
5. Minor Prophets

There are five categories, but only two will be listed for now:

1. Law
    Genesis
    Exodus
    Leviticus
    Numbers
    Deuteronomy

2. History
    Joshua
    Judges
    Ruth
    1-2 Samuel
    1-2 Kings
    1-2 Chronicles
    Ezra 1-6
    Esther
    Ezra 7-10
    Nehemiah

These books are listed in Bible sequence and in chronological order, with the exception of Esther. The book of Esther is the last book in Bible **sequence**, however, it should be read after the reading of the first six chapters of Ezra.

In these first 17 books is the entire history of the Old Testament. For my own study I think this was the most welcome discovery. **The history of the Old Testament is not 39 books long, it is 17 books long. The other 22 books fit historically within these 17 books.** As you will notice, I have Exodus through Nehemiah, for the Old Testament, under the Mosaical Dispensation, instead of Malachi, the last book in Bible sequence. Old Testament history ends with the book of Nehemiah.

Although the first five books are called the Law, or Torah, they are very much a part of the historical books. These books record the beginnings: of the world, of man and the beginning of the Israelite Nation.

In taking the history of these 17 books and dividing it into periods, we have the whole of the Old Testament into segments which can be easily studied and understood. This is where the use of the clock comes in. I have associated all that I study of the Old Testament with the clock, and it works beautifully for me.

In the use of the clock idea I have experienced failures as well as successes. The failures resulted when I attempted to expand the study of each period before the whole of each clock was put to memory. **The main purpose of the clock is to enable us to grasp the Old Testament as a whole.** It is only after we can see it as a whole that we are able to fit books, people, places and things in their rightful places. So for 3 years students left my classes far short of the goal I had set for them.

Therefore, it is of utmost importance to put to memory all the periods of the first clock. Copy that clock, with pencil and paper, until you know the periods as well as you know the numbers on that clock. When you have done that you have an idea of what the Old Testament is all about, and you are ready to learn where to go to study those periods.

Only after you know the periods should you go to the next clock. Make a new clock, put the periods on it and then add the books. In this way you keep all of it before you at all times. **Proceed in this manner with each clock, always in order, the period, the book, the people and geography, until you are able to put all four clocks on one clock by memory.** Now you are an independent student of the Old Testament.

If you start at 1 o'clock with an in-depth study of that period, it will be a long time before you will have a grasp of the whole of the Old Testament. My successes came only after two years of experience of learning how best to use the clocks.

- STUDY NOTES -

II. THE ESSENCE OF TIME CLOCKS

THE PERIODS CLOCK
The Periods of Old Testament History

Start at 1 o'clock and read clockwise

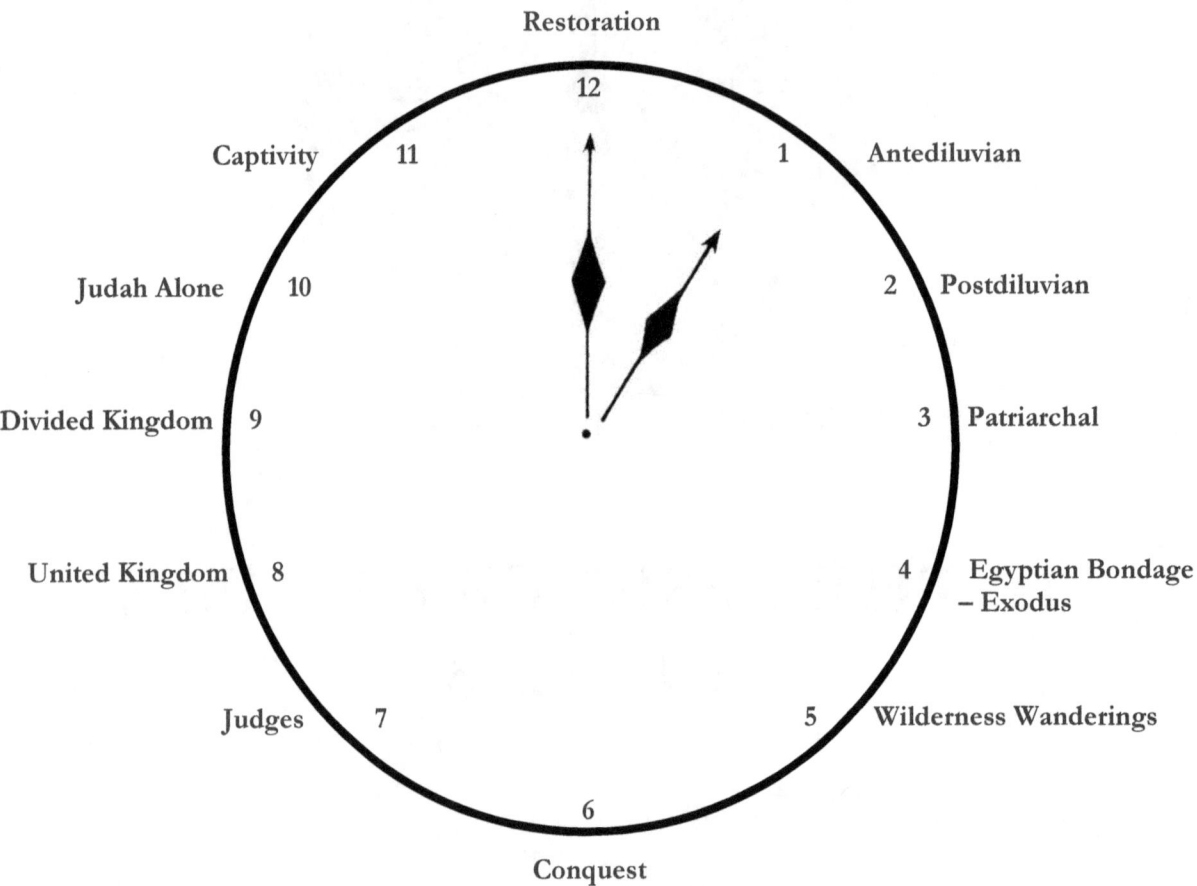

THE PERIODS CLOCK DETAIL

On this first clock we have the entire Old Testament, divided into periods. All we want to do for now is to become familiar with these period names and what they mean.

Start at 1 o'clock and read clockwise

12 o'clock - Restoration
Jews restored to their land

11 o'clock - Captivity
Judah in Babylonian Captivity

1 o'clock - Antediluvian
"Before the flood"

10 o'clock - Judah Alone
Assyrians take Israel, Judah left alone

2 o'clock - Postdiluvian
"After the Flood"

9 o'clock - Divided Kingdom
Kingdom divided
Two kingdoms, Israel - Judah

3 o'clock - Patriarchal
"Father rule"-social & spiritual

8 o'clock - United Kingdom
All the people united under one king

4 o'clock - Egypt - Bondage
Israelites in Egypt and the Exodus

7 o'clock - Judges
Israelites led by Judges

5 o'clock - Wanderings
38 years in the wilderness

6 o'clock - Conquest
Conquest of the Promised Land

THE BOOKS CLOCK
The Books Covering the Twelve Old Testament Periods

Start at 1 o'clock and read clockwise

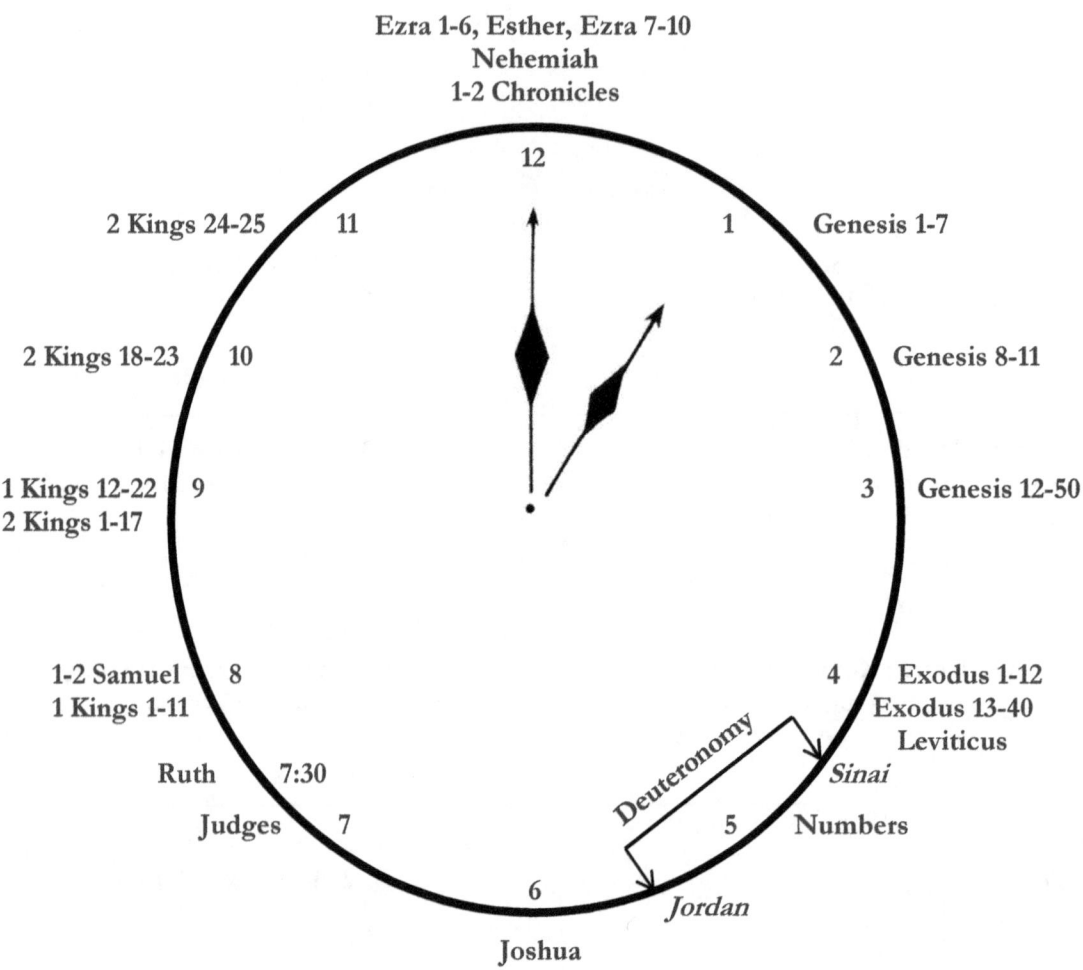

THE BOOKS CLOCK DETAIL

This second clock shows the books which cover the periods of Old Testament history. These are the books of Law and History. This clock will give a general working understanding of just where to go to study certain subjects.

The names are from the Greek and are so named from the subject of the book. Bible is from the Greek word "biblos," meaning "the book."

Start at 1 o'clock and read clockwise

12 o'clock
Ezra 1-6, Esther, Ezra 7-10, Nehemiah
Captivity ends; rebuilding of temple, also wall of Jerusalem
Ezra compiles 1-2 Chronicles

11 o'clock - 2 Kings 24-25
Judah taken into Babylonian Captivity

1 o'clock - Genesis 1-7
Genesis means "beginnings"
From creation to flood

10 o'clock - 2 Kings 18-23
History of last kings of Judah only
Israel has been taken captive by Assyria

2 o'clock - Genesis 8-11
From flood to call of Abraham

9 o'clock – 1 Kings 12-22; 2 Kings 1-17
Kingdom divides
Rehoboam, king of Judah, Southern Kingdom
Jeroboam, king of Israel, Northern Kingdom

3 o'clock - Genesis 12-50
From call of Abraham to death of Joseph

8 o'clock - 1-2 Samuel; 1 Kings 1-11
Birth and life of Samuel; life of King Saul, of King David and King Solomon

4 o'clock - Exodus 1-12, 13-40
Leviticus
Exodus means "departure"
Leviticus means "pertaining to the Levites"
Bondage - Journey to Mt. Sinai

Deuteronomy means "Law repeated."
Repeat of events of 4 and 5 o'clock.

7:30 o'clock - Ruth
Introduction of the family of David

5 o'clock - Numbers Numbering of the Army of Israel at Sinai and Jordan

7 o'clock – Judges
The people led by Judges

6 o'clock - Joshua
Conquest of Canaan, led by Joshua

THE V.I.P. CLOCK

V.I.P.'s of the Old Testament
The lineage of Christ is underlined

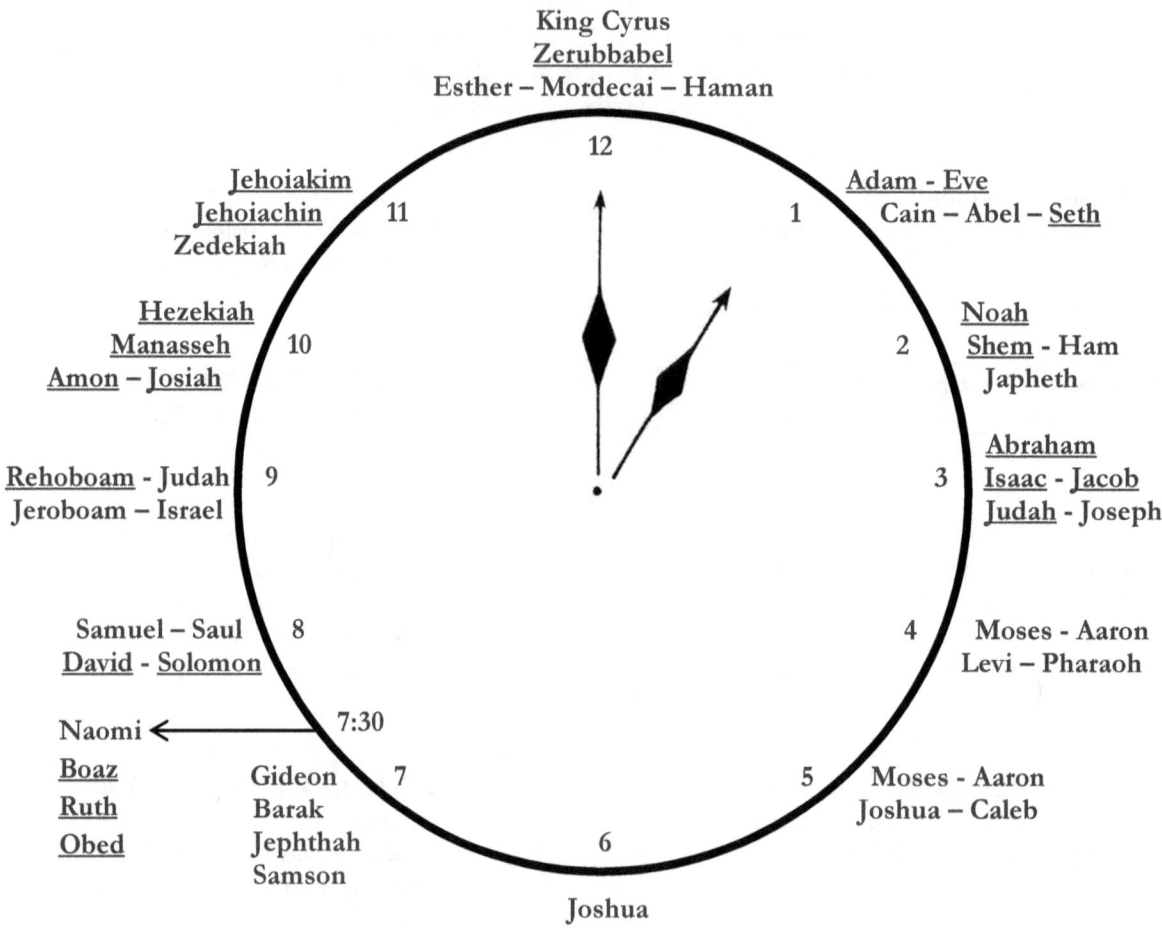

THE V.I.P. CLOCK DETAIL

This third clock shows the V.I.P.'s (Very Important Persons) which cover the periods of Old Testament history. This clock will give a general understanding of who the main Bible characters are in each period of time.

Start at 1 o'clock and read clockwise

12 o'clock
King Cyrus of Persia allowed the Restoration.
Zerubbabel, grandson of Jehoiachin, led first group back to Jerusalem
Esther & Mordecai save the Jews from extermination by Haman

11 o'clock
Jehoiakim - Captivity begins; **Jehoiachin** taken to Babylon; **Zedekiah**, last king of Judah

10 o'clock
Hezekiah, Manasseh, Amon and **Josiah**, some of the last kings of Judah Alone

9 o'clock
Rehoboam, son of Solomon, king of Judah
Jeroboam, prophesied king of ten tribes of the kingdom of Israel

8 o'clock
Samuel makes transition from Judges to Kings
Saul, first king, **David**, his son
Solomon, kings of all Israel

7:30 o'clock- **Naomi**, mother-in-law of **Ruth**
Boaz, husband of **Ruth**, their child
Obed, grandfather of **David**

7 o'clock
Gideon, Barak, Jephthah and **Samson** are the four Judges mentioned in the hall of faith in Hebrews 11

1 o'clock
Adam, **Eve** and their three recorded sons, **Cain, Abel** and Seth

2 o'clock
Noah and his sons, **Shem, Ham** and **Japheth**

3 o'clock
Abraham, Isaac, Jacob and **Judah** progenitors of the chosen people

4 o'clock
Moses, Lawgiver
Aaron, High Priest
Levi, Priestly tribe
Pharaoh, king of Egypt

5 o'clock
Moses - Aaron.
Joshua and **Caleb**, the two faithful spies out of twelve

6 o'clock
Joshua led the people in the conquest of Canaan

V.I.P.'s of Old Testament History

It is of great importance that we keep the Bible characters in their rightful places in the history of the chosen people of God. **God's plan is so wrapped up in some of these Bible characters and to confuse their order is to confuse the orderly plan of God for the redemption of man.**

We must understand that **Abraham was before Moses**, because God gave one of the first most important promises of the Bible to Abraham, "that in him all the families of the earth would be blessed."

Then some 430 years later He gave a set of very important laws to Moses for His people. The Apostle Paul wrote in his letter to the Galatians that the giving of the law to Moses could not disannul the promise given to Abraham. **So in this way we see that the Messianic plan does not have its foundation in the Law of Moses, but rather, the Law of Moses takes its rightful place in the Messianic plan.** We go back before Abraham, to the Garden of Eden, for the first hint of the Messiah; His purpose, then, is founded in the Abrahamic Covenant.

So we see that it is important to know that Abraham was before Moses. **Also, the numerous lineages are in the scriptures for the purpose of knowing where the different characters appear in Bible history.** "All scripture is profitable," Paul said to Timothy.

This third clock gives only a few of the Bible characters to put to memory. You will find that after a little while it is not a matter of memorizing as much as just remembering in which period the different characters appear. **You will want to make note of others as they relate to the ones given, as you begin your in-depth study of each period.**

It is also of importance to know who is of the lineage of Christ. To give examples of this:

a. **Joseph** is one of the most familiar characters of the Old Testament. His life is taught from the first grade on, yet he is not of the lineage of Christ. It was one of his brothers, about whom we know very little, Judah, through whom the Messiah was to come.

b. **Moses** is the main character of three of the first five books of the Bible; the man in whom the entire Jewish nation found their belief, yet he is not of the lineage of the Messiah.

c. **Joshua** took over the leadership of that great new nation of chosen people and led them into the Promised Land in fulfillment of one phase of the Abrahamic Covenant, yet he is not of the lineage of the Messiah.

The most familiar, faithful characters are often thought to be of the Messianic lineage. The lineage of Christ is found in:

Genesis 5:3-32; 11:10-27;
Matthew 1:2-16;
Luke 3:23-38, among others.

THE BIBLE LANDS CLOCK
Bible Lands of the Old Testament

Start at 1 o'clock and read clockwise

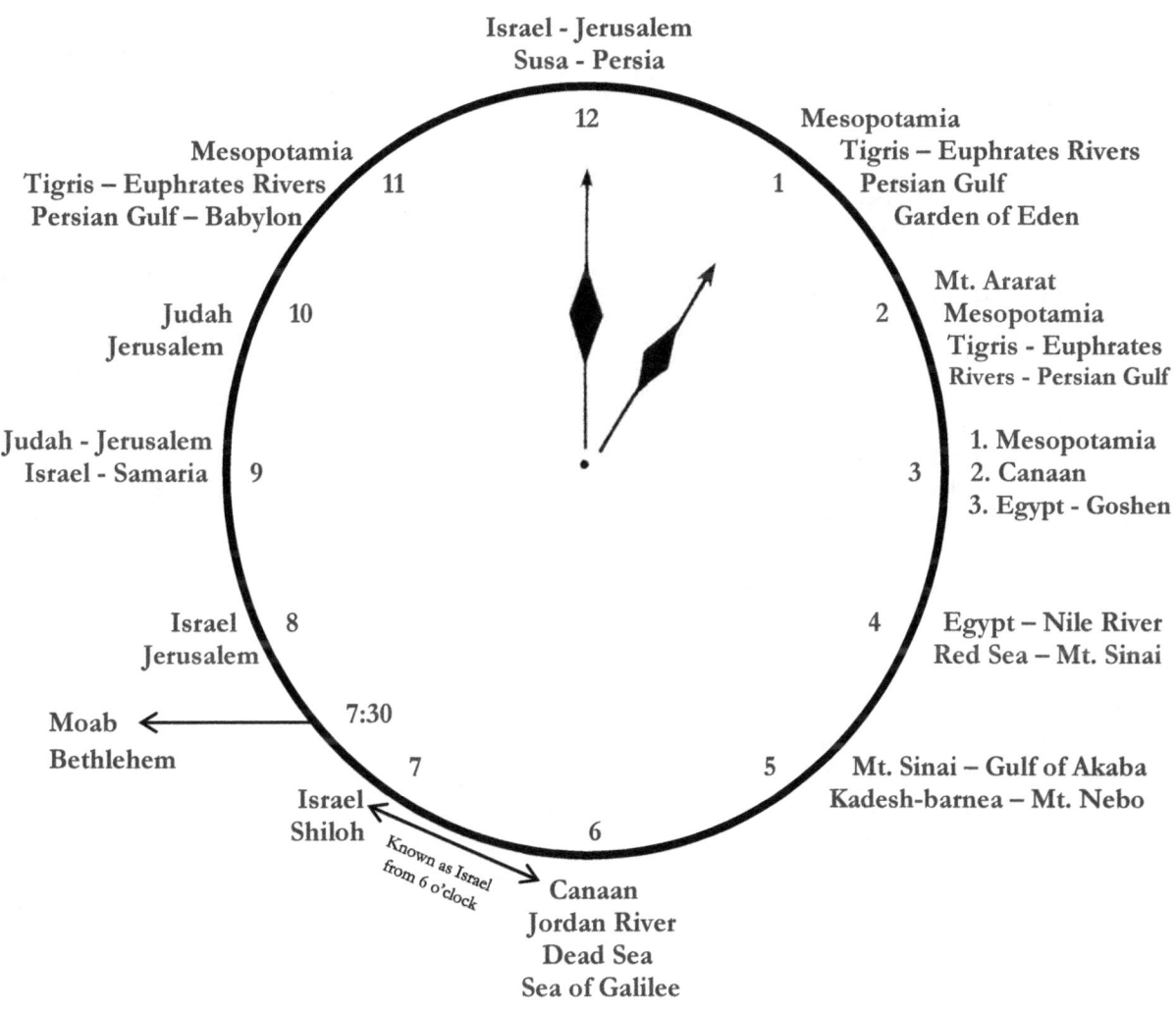

Bible Lands of Old Testament History

There are two thoughts on geography which sum up the importance I place on this most vital and most neglected area of Bible study:

a. "Geography is the eye of history"

b. "As geography without history seemeth a carcass without motion; so history without geography wandereth as a vagrant without a certain habitation." Authors unknown.

The first of these two thoughts is probably very familiar to you. However, I wonder if you have really considered what it says. **For me to try to teach the Bible without maps is like asking you to take a trip with me through the Bible lands blindfolded.** I know you would refuse to take that trip with me. Neither should you agree to go through the Bible with me blindfolded; that is exactly what you are doing if you don't insist on maps. In this study there is at least one map for each period. We want to see where we've been and where we're going. Geography is truly the eye of history.

The second thought on geography is probably my favorite. Two pictures come to my mind when I read it. One is the perennial desert scene with the carcass of a steer; absolutely no life in this picture. The opposite of this picture is the sight of an ant hill, where there seems to be no rhyme or reason for all the coming and going. So it is with me in the study of the Bible without my maps. People are coming and going to places that make no sense to me unless I locate them on the map. **Geography truly has no life without people, and history without geography certainly is a mass of confusion.** You will find that geography will increase your speed of learning one hundred fold, and nothing can grasp the memory of what you've learned from you.

Now that you've decided to include geography in your study of the Bible, drawing your own maps is of great value. They need to be very simple and you need have only the information on each map for your immediate study. Commercial maps have too much information on them and only detract from your train of thought. I make many maps of the same area. One might have just mountains, or rivers, or main travel routes; for the purpose of having these certain things stand out vividly in my memory. **I must warn you to be sure you have your information correct before you start drawing your maps because it will stay with you so well that you will find it hard to forget the wrong you've learned.**

The maps in this study are most simple. You might even want to trace them at the beginning until they become familiar to you. **Learning to draw your own maps also helps tremendously when you are asked at the last minute to teach a class of any kind.** You just walk over to a blackboard and make the Bible come to life before your class.

As with any area, the Bible lands have marks of distinction which do not change. These serve as the framework within which you will build information. These marks of distinction are given as we go around the clock.

As you will notice on this fourth clock, 1 o'clock and 2 o'clock take place in the same general location, the so-called cradle of creation. The land is called Mesopotamia which means "'the land between the rivers": the Tigris and Euphrates Rivers. These two rivers empty into the Persian Gulf. So we have at **1 o'clock** Mesopotamia, Tigris and Euphrates Rivers and the Persian Gulf. Somewhere in the area where these two rivers join was the Garden of Eden.

At **2 o'clock** we find the ark resting on Mt. Ararat, about half way between the Black Sea and the Caspian Sea, above the country of Armenia, some 20,000 feet above sea level. After leaving the ark the descendants of Noah migrate back down to "the land between the rivers." So for 2 o'clock there is Mt. Ararat, the Tigris and Euphrates Rivers, the Persian Gulf and Mesopotamia.

3 o'clock begins in the southernmost part of Mesopotamia at the head waters of the Persian Gulf. The land is Chaldea and the city is Ur. Terah, father of Abraham, takes his family and moves north to the city of Haran in Padan-Aram on the Euphrates River, in the area where that river flows closest to the Mediterranean Sea. Then it is from Haran that Abraham leaves for Canaan with his wife, Sarah, and his nephew, Lot. In Canaan, Abraham built an altar first at Shechem, then Bethel and Beer-sheba as he traveled down through the land. In time he went down into Egypt. When he returned to Canaan, he lived in both Beer-sheba and Hebron. Long after the death of Abraham, Jacob with his family moved down into Egypt in an area called Goshen.

At **4 o'clock** we find the descendants of Abraham under Egyptian bondage. In Egypt we find the longest river system in the world, the Nile, being some 4,000 miles long. As the Israelites come out of Egypt they cross the west arm of the Red Sea, otherwise known as the Gulf of Suez. They travel down the east side of the Gulf of Suez to Mt. Sinai.

At **5 o'clock** the people are still at Mt. Sinai. When they leave Mt. Sinai they travel up the west side of the east arm of the Red Sea, otherwise known as the Gulf of Akaba. Their general headquarters for most of the wanderings is Kadesh-barnea, at the southernmost end of the land of Canaan. At the end of the wanderings, Moses dies on Mt. Nebo on the eastern side of the Dead Sea in the area where the Jordan River flows into the Dead Sea.

At **6 o'clock** the Israelites conquer the land of Canaan. The land on the east of the Jordan was conquered at 5 o'clock. On the west of the Jordan the land taken was from Dan in the north to Beer-sheba in the south. The landmarks then are the Sea of Galilee, Jordan River and the Dead Sea.

At **7 o'clock** Canaan is known as the land of Israel.

At **7:30 o'clock** Elimelech and Naomi go to Moab: Naomi and Ruth return to Bethlehem.

At **8 o'clock** David captures the city of Jerusalem and makes it his headquarters.

At **9 o'clock,** as the Kingdom divides, Jerusalem is capital city of the southern kingdom of Judah, and Samaria is made capital city of the northern kingdom of Israel.

At **10 o'clock** only Judah remains and the city of Jerusalem remains the religious center.

At **11 o'clock** Judah is taken captive by the Babylonians and the people are taken to Babylon in Mesopotamia.

At **12 o'clock** Cyrus, first king of Persia, allows the "Jews" to return to Jerusalem to rebuild Jerusalem and the temple. Later, King Darius, third king of Persia, builds the palace at Susa. Susa becomes the capital city of Persia. Esther lived in Susa as queen of Ahasuerus, fourth king of Persia.

Old Testament history ends at 12 o'clock. As you draw your maps be sure to catalogue them in the correct period section. As with any other notes you catalogue in the correct period section, they remain in your memory that way.

When you start the study of any of these periods, have your map in front of you. Most important of all, have your Bible open in front of you.

- STUDY NOTES -

- STUDY NOTES -

- STUDY NOTES -

III. 1 o'clock
ANTEDILUVIAN

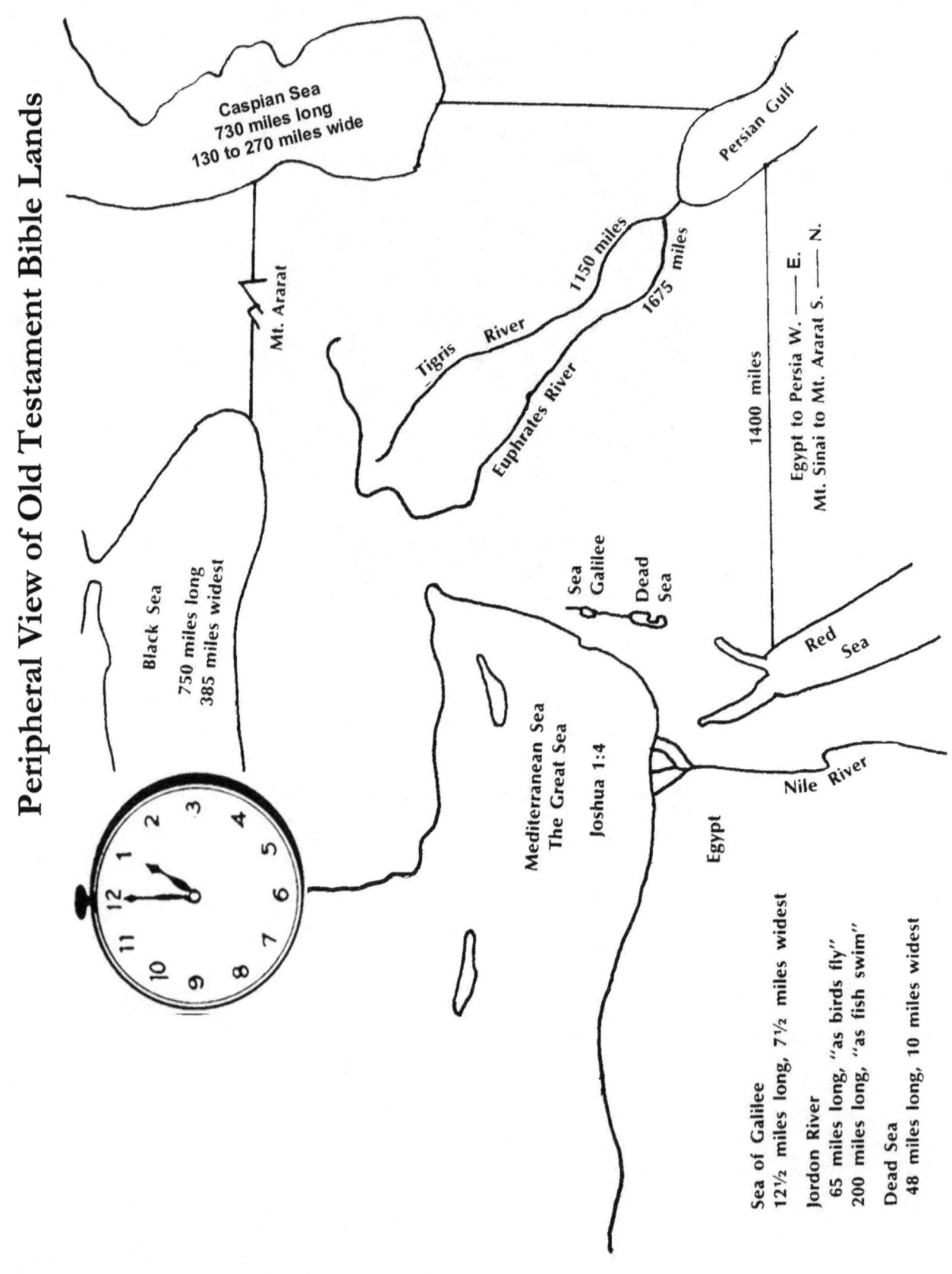

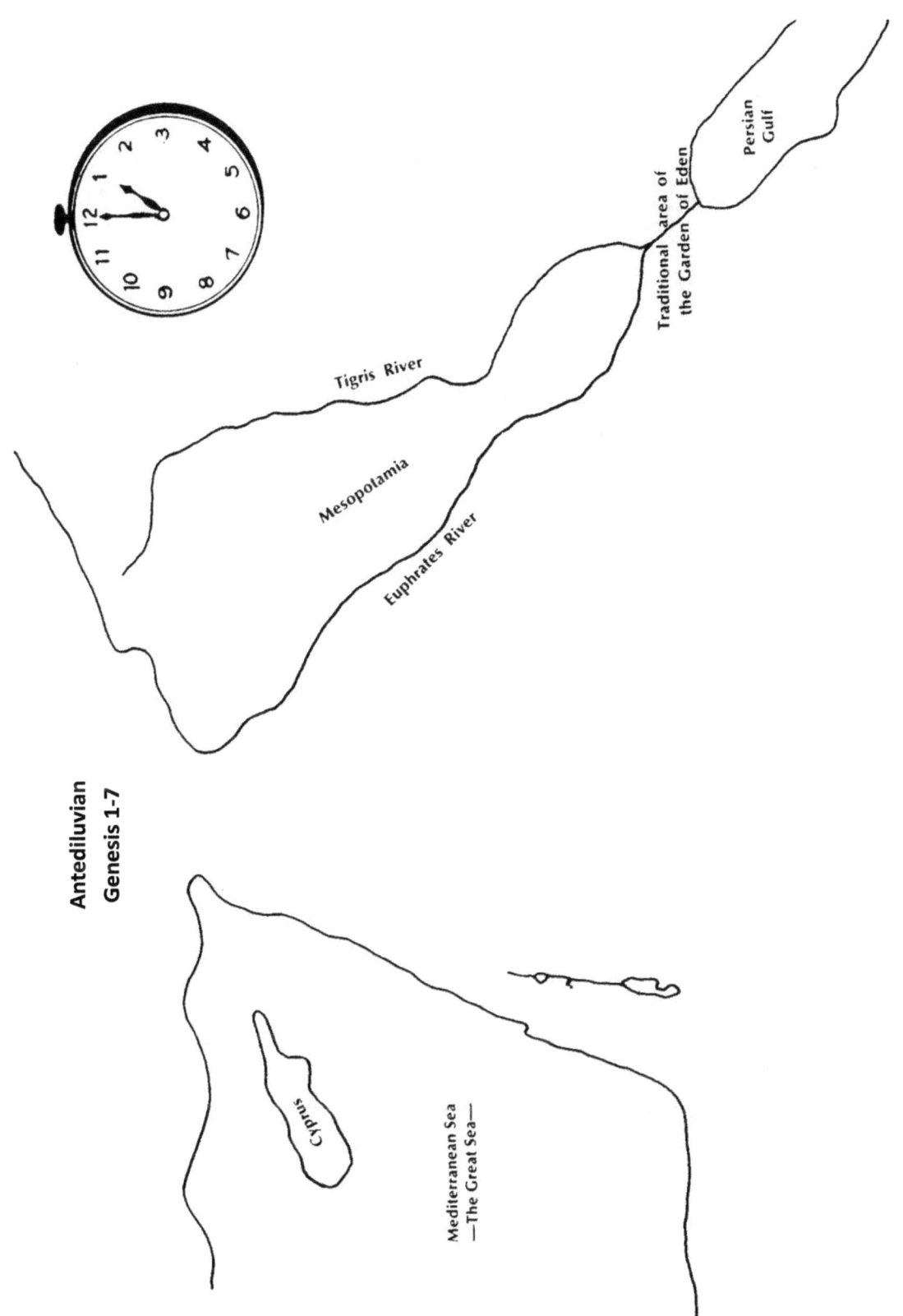

Geography

In the section of introduction we looked at the map with peripheral vision. We saw on that map the outside boundaries of the land in which the history of the Old Testament takes place. However, at the beginning of each period we will be narrowing our vision to a particular area of the map. **Only those places pertinent to the immediate study will be shown on these maps.** We do want always to think about the whole map while we are working in a specific section; just as we will be thinking of the whole clock as we study each period. In this way we get into the habit of knowing where and how a particular study fits into the whole of the Bible.

The Bible itself has very little information of the geography before the flood. There are four rivers mentioned in Genesis 2:11-14, the **Pison, Gihon, Tigris and Euphrates**. Of course, two of these are very familiar to us; the Tigris and Euphrates. It is the land between these two rivers that is called Mesopotamia, meaning "the land between the rivers." The Tigris and Euphrates flow together from about one hundred miles above the Persian Gulf. Somewhere in this vicinity was the Garden of Eden.

Antediluvian
"before the flood"
Genesis 1-7

Although it is not the purpose of the Bible to record general history, the Bible is historical in nature. **In the first 7 chapters of the Bible we have the world's only record of the creation of all things.** The Bible does not present the creation in theory, but in fact. "In the beginning God created the heavens and the earth." Man's struggle to understand how this was accomplished does not, nor will it ever, alter the fact of Genesis 1:1. Also, after reading the opinion of many scholarly men I see no reason to labor over the fact that God accomplished the creation of all things in seven 24 hour days.

After preparing the earth for habitation God created man, Genesis 1:27. He then made the woman from the flesh and bones of the man, Genesis 2:21-23. This is also presented as a fact. There is absolutely no need to labor this point. I accept it exactly as it is stated. I have no intention of watering these facts down nor will I entertain any dilution of these facts from anyone else. I will accept the simple truths of the Bible and struggle with the difficult.

In the third chapter of Genesis we have recorded the conditions under which **Adam and Eve** sinned and set in motion the scheme of the redemption of man. This, of course, is the primary purpose of the Bible. Here, at the very beginning, is the place to start our study of the Bible in order to understand God's plan for the redemption of man back to Himself.

For this study we will use varied frameworks within which we gather the knowledge of the Old Testament. One of these will be the use of years, and in doing this we need to choose one authority on the **chronology of the Bible** and stick with that one, only as a matter of convenience. I use the chronology as calculated by Archbishop Ussher in 1650 A.D. In his calculation of Genesis 5, this period before the flood is some 1656 years in time. There are more years covered in this one period than there is from 4 o'clock through 12 o'clock to the advent of Christ. The years are usually calculated to be 2500 from the creation to the giving of the law on Mt. Sinai and 1500 from the giving of the law on Mt. Sinai to the birth of Christ. It will be within this framework that this work will progress.

Any study about the Bible should not be undertaken without an open Bible in front of you. To know the will of God there is no getting around reading every verse of every chapter of every book for yourself. **Years can be wasted in reading material about the Bible, because in the end there is no substitute for the knowledge of the Bible itself.** I speak from experience.

For the study of this first period consider the following outline. You will want to make further notes of details.

I. The material order:

Genesis 1:2-5:   First Day: Light

Genesis 1:6-8:   Second Day: Firmament

Genesis 1:9-13: Third Day: Dry land and vegetation

Genesis 1:14-19: Fourth Day: Sun, moon and stars

II The sentient order:

Genesis 1:20-23: Fifth Day: Sea and winged animals

Genesis 1:24-31: Sixth Day: Beast – cattle Man made in the image of God and Christ Genesis 1:27

Genesis 2:1-3:   Seventh Day: God rested from the work of the Creation.

→ **Sight, hearing, smell, taste, touch**

After God created the world, He created man. He then made the woman of the bone and flesh of the man, 2:23. It was God who instituted the home, with one man and one woman. No matter what man does later, God's plan from the beginning was one man for one woman. Anything else is foreign to God.

Genesis 3-5   Sin enters the world

In their first home, the **Garden of Eden**, Adam and Eve fail to see the importance of obeying God's command, and God sends them out from his presence. Before he does, however, he initiates his plan to redeem man, Genesis 3:15. You will want to obtain a thorough understanding of this verse as it is vital to the building of the Messianic theme of the Old Testament. Genesis 3:15 is the first of many verses that point to the One who was to be the Savior of the world. We must understand the significance of one to be born of the seed of the woman, without benefit of the man; see Genesis 12:3 and Galatians 3:16. The thread of Christ runs throughout the Old Testament. **This is why we need to obtain a knowledge of the Old Testament to the degree that we can lay down the history of the Israelite people and glean out from that knowledge all those things pertaining to Christ and His church.** This is the ultimate purpose of the study of the Old Testament.

Along with Adam and Eve the Bible records the names of three of their sons. They are Cain, Abel and Seth. Most everyone is familiar with Cain and Abel, but very few know about Seth, and Seth is the son through whom Christ comes, Genesis 5.

The circumstances surrounding Enoch, seventh from Adam, is said to be the first hint of immortality and the only one before the flood. Elijah is an example of this after the flood and before Christ. So in every age God has given man a sign that this earthly life is not all there is.

Genesis 6-7   Universal wickedness

As the years went by, man grew more and more wicked until, as it is written, "Every imagination of the thoughts of his heart was only evil continually." God said, "I will destroy man, whom I have created, from the face of the earth. . . "

He called **Noah**, a man of the line of Seth, to build an ark in preparation for the flood for the purpose of saving a remnant of the people.

It appears from Genesis 6:3, that God gave the people of the world 120 years in which to decide their own fate, so you can see that God waited patiently for the people to return to following Him; read I Peter 3:20. Noah and his wife, their three sons and their wives were the only ones who believed God when He said He would destroy all that He had created from the face of the earth.

Make your own notes and add them to the workbook under the correct time period. This study will only serve as an outline and will not deprive you of reading and becoming familiar with the Bible itself.

- STUDY NOTES -

- STUDY NOTES -

IV. 2 o'clock
POSTDILUVIAN

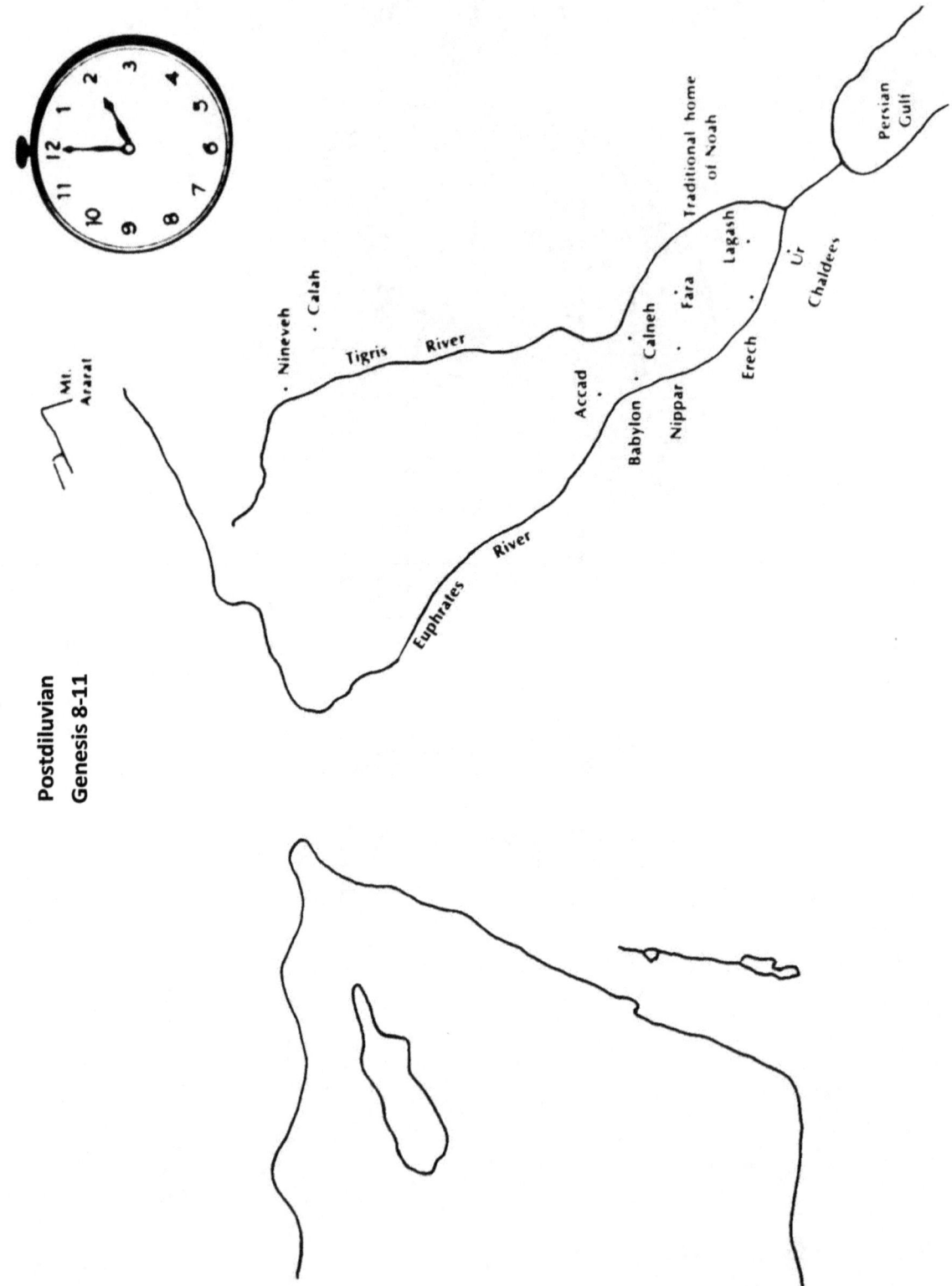

Postdiluvian
Genesis 8-11

Geography

As 2 o'clock opens we find Noah with his family still in the ark waiting for the waters to recede. The ark is resting on **Mt. Ararat.** Mt. Ararat is about half way between the Black Sea and the Caspian Sea, above the country of Armenia. Mt. Ararat rises some 20,000 feet above sea level.

Throughout the some 400 years to follow, before the call of Abraham, the descendants of Noah migrate back down to the "land between the rivers," Mesopotamia. In time we find Nimrod building great cities, among them being **Babel, Erech, Accad** and **Calneh** in the land of Shinar. Also Nineveh and Calah in what was later to be called Assyria.

As we will see at 3 o'clock, **Ur** is the home of Abraham.

Postdiluvian
"after the flood"
Genesis 8-11
Noah to Abraham

Postdiluvian is that period of time from the landing of the ark on Mt. Ararat to the call of Abraham.

Noah and his family were in the ark a little over a year, Genesis 7:11; 8:13-16. **The first seven months included the forty days of rain and the time spent on the flood waters. The next five months were spent on the mountain waiting for the water to recede.**

The first thing Noah did after leaving the ark was build an altar to **sacrifice** to God. God was pleased with Noah's sacrifice and at this time He set a rainbow in the cloud and made a covenant that He would never again destroy the earth with water, Genesis 9:8-17. Now is the time to remember where to read about the covenant of the rainbow; right after the flood.

Noah's three sons were Shem, Ham and Japheth. The selection of Shem to carry the Messianic lineage forward was the outcome of Noah's drunkenness, Genesis 9:20-27.

In the years to come Noah's family began to migrate back down to Mesopotamia. The lineage of Noah's three sons are given in Genesis 10, as is the origin of the nations. This spreading out over the earth resulted from the effort to build the tower of Babel, Genesis 11:1-9; which occurred about 100 years after the flood in the time of Peleg, fourth generation from Shem, Genesis 10:25.

The time from the scattering of the people to the call of Abraham, then, was about 326 years; time of which we have very little information.

These lineages given from time to time, nine of which are in the book of Genesis, serve as excellent frameworks within which we can build our knowledge of the Old Testament characters. In the lineage of Noah and sons, Genesis 10, **Nimrod** stands out as a builder of great cities and seems to have been one of the monarchs of the city kingdoms of his day. Two of these cities, Babylon and Nineveh, will be very prominent cities in our studies of the periods from 9 o'clock through 11 o'clock.

In Genesis 10:6 we see that Ham had four sons. Of these sons the Israelites contend mostly with the descendants of Canaan and Mizraim: the descendants of Mizraim, the Egyptians, at 4 o'clock and the descendants of Canaan in the conquest at 6 o'clock. On most commercial maps you will see the name of Mizraim instead of Egypt or on some both names are used.

In Genesis 5 there are ten generations named from Adam to Noah and in Genesis 10 there are ten generations named from Noah to Abraham. Then according to Matthew 1:17 there are fourteen generations from 3 o'clock to 8 o'clock; fourteen generations from 8 o'clock to 11 o'clock and fourteen generations from 11 o'clock to Christ. Again, a good framework within which to build information.

These first two periods bring home the fact of the brevity of the Bible; eleven chapters covering a period of 2,000 years. However, the very foundation for our belief in God and His word are in these chapters. These are the chapters that our modern critics want to do away with, as far as their historical value is concerned; "theistic evolutionists" they call themselves. They want to hang on to their belief in God, but explain the creation in an evolutionary manner.

However, the New Testament refers over and over to the varied activities of the people of these years, lending credence to them as historical events. Paul refers to the serpent beguiling Eve, in 2 Corinthians 11:3 and also Adam, in 1 Timothy 2:14. He refers to the creation of the man and then the woman being made from the man, in 1 Corinthians 11:8. Cain and Abel are referred to as actual historical characters in Matthew 23:35; Hebrews 11:4; 1 John 3:12 and Jude 11. The names of Abel, Enoch and Noah are recorded in the "hall of faith" in Hebrews 11. Peter refers to the flood as actually happening, 1 Peter 3:20.

As for me, **"I believe that every word of every verse in every chapter of every book of the Bible is from the mind of God and it says what He means and He means what He says."**

Then for a birds-eye view of 2 o'clock there is:

a. The ark on Mt. Ararat;
b. The covenant of the rainbow;
c. The building of the tower of Babel.

You will want to read Genesis 8-11 and make your own notes and place them in your workbook at 2 o'clock.

- STUDY NOTES -

- STUDY NOTES -

- STUDY NOTES -

V. 3 o'clock
PATRIARCHAL

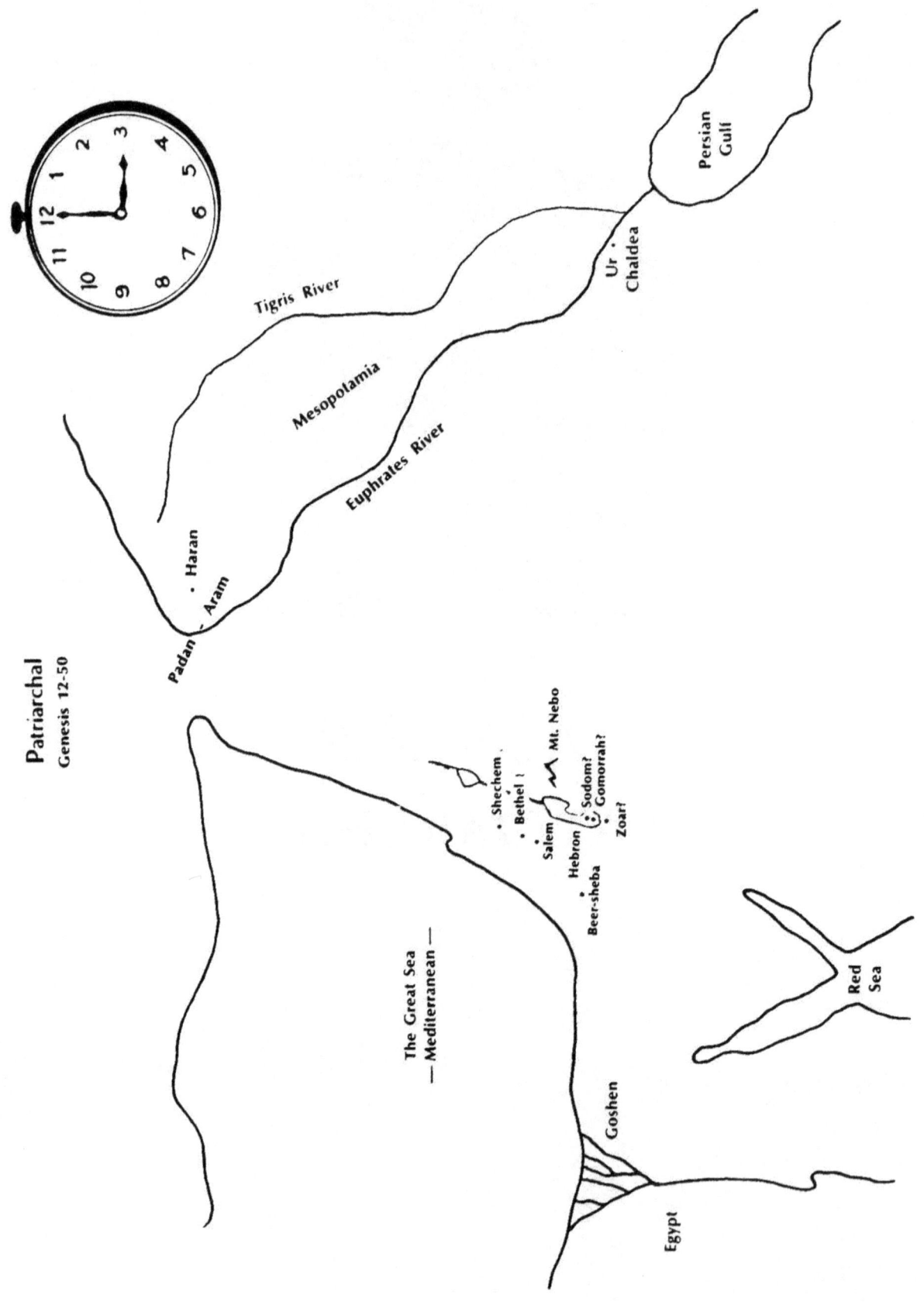

Geography

As you will notice, 3 o'clock opens in the same area of 1 o'clock and 2 o'clock. Terah lived, with his three sons Abraham, Nahor and Haran, in the city of Ur of the Chaldees, at the headwaters of the Persian Gulf. Terah took his family and moved about six hundred miles north, to the city of **Haran** in **Padan-Aram**, on the east side of the Euphrates River.

It was not until after the death of Terah that Abraham takes his wife Sarah and nephew Lot and starts down through the land of Canaan. Their first stop was Sichem, later called **Shechem**. We read more about Shechem in Genesis 34. They move on down to **Bethel**, where years later, Jacob stops on his way to Haran, Genesis 28.

Then Abraham and Sarah go to Egypt. On their return they go back to Bethel. The herdsmen of Abraham and the herdsmen of Lot argue over the land and Lot moves to the area of **Sodom** and **Gomorrah**.

Abraham then moves to **Hebron**.

Abraham pays tithes to Melchizedek, king and priest of **Salem**.

After the destruction of Sodom and Gomorrah, Lot goes into the mountain city of **Zoar**.

Later, Abraham moved to **Beersheba**. It was to Beersheba that Rebekah came to live as Isaac's wife.

In Genesis 37 Joseph is sold by his brothers and taken down into Egypt. Later, in Genesis 46, Jacob moves the whole family to Goshen in **Lower Egypt**.

Patriarchal

Genesis 12-50

Abraham to Joseph

Under the patriarchal system, the father had rule over all, born or bought, social and spiritual, in his family. This system goes back to the very beginning, but for this period we are specifically interested in the patriarchs **Abraham, Isaac, Jacob and Joseph.**

At 1 o'clock we have the beginning of all that God created. In this 3 o'clock period we have another very important beginning. We can see very clearly just where the chosen people of God of the Old Testament had their beginning. A people who are to highlight all that the Old Testament teaches. In the lives of some of these people we see the **redemptive plan** of God unfold. This is why it is of utmost importance that we see them in their chronological order.

For the most part, Abraham's life begins in Genesis 12, however it is in Genesis 11:26-32 that we find where he comes from. On a separate page I have a diagram of this family. I believe it gives a more impressive picture of the interrelationship of Abraham's family. Along with that diagram are some interesting facts concerning this interrelationship that have to do with people we will be meeting throughout this study of the Old Testament.

In Genesis 12:1-3 we have one of the most important promises of the Old Testament. It is most important that we understand it, because it serves as an ultimate goal of the people of the Old Testament as well as for all of us today. In letting the Bible be its own interpreter, this promise serves as the basis of the understanding of when the Old Covenant ends and the New Covenant begins.

The promise is three-fold. God promises Abraham:

a. to show him a land that would ultimately be his **inheritance**, Genesis 12:7; 17:1-8;

b. that He would make of him **a great nation** of people, Genesis 22:17; from which kings would come, Genesis 17:6.

c. "and in him all the nations of the earth would be **blessed**."

It is in the land of Canaan, at 6 o'clock, that the first promise is fulfilled. It is in Isaac, Jacob and from Jacob's twelve sons that the second promise is fulfilled. Last and most important of all, it is in Jesus Christ and His church that the last of this three-fold promise has its fulfillment. The adding of the Law of Moses could not disannul this promise given to Abraham; study Galatians 3. It is in the establishment of the Church of our Lord, Acts 2, that this promise is fully realized.

In the further study of this period it would be profitable to designate the chapters in which we study the four main characters.

Abraham............Genesis 11:26 - 25:8

Isaac............. Genesis 21:1 - 35:29

Jacob............. Genesis 25:21 - 49:33

Joseph............ Genesis 30:22 - 50:26

As you can see there are only twelve chapters to read to know the life of Abraham. **Sit down with pencil and paper and from the Bible itself make a good outline of your own of his life and slip it into your workbook at 3 o'clock.** As you do this it will make such a mark on your memory that you will never forget it.

You just can't possibly see Abraham anywhere except at 3 o'clock. As you follow Abraham's life you should be sure to have an extra sheet of paper handy because you will want to do the same thing with Isaac and of course their lives overlap. You will find you are half way through the life of Isaac when you finish with Abraham. In doing this with any or all the characters of each period you will have a collection that could be worth life eternal for you and others of whom it is your responsibility to teach. Read Hosea 4:6.

One thing should be made clear at this time. Even though the life of Joseph is much more pronounced in detail than any of his brothers, and though he's the favorite son of Jacob's favorite wife, he is not the son of Jacob through whom the Messiah is to come. **The lineage of Christ is through Judah, fourth son of Jacob by Leah, of whom we know but little.** Joseph was the eleventh son of Jacob, by Rachel.

Within the lives of these patriarchs are some of the most familiar stories of the Bible:

a. Abraham's faith shown in his willingness to offer his son, **Isaac**, on the altar, knowing that somehow God would raise him up.

b. Isaac, with his wife Rebekah and their two sons, **Esau and Jacob.** Esau sells his birthright to Jacob for some pottage Jacob had prepared. Rebekah and Jacob then deceive Isaac in bestowing the birthright on Jacob instead of Esau, the eldest. All of this in fulfillment of Genesis 25:23.

c. Jacob is himself deceived when later in the city of Haran he works for 7 years for his Uncle Laban for the privilege of marrying his younger daughter. On the night of the wedding, **Leah**, elder sister of **Rachel**, is put into the wedding tent by Laban. Jacob has to work another 7 years for Rachel.

d. **Joseph**, first son of Rachel, is shown to be his father's favorite son. **Jacob shows this in the making of the special coat of many colors.** This, along with some peculiar dreams Joseph was having, caused the other sons to be jealous. In their jealousy they sold Joseph and he was taken down into Egypt. In time, Joseph became second in command under the Pharaoh of Egypt. In a time of famine in Canaan, all the family of Jacob, 70 souls, just counting the males, enter Egypt. There they grow into a nation of over three million people. The second phase of the promise to Abraham is fulfilled.

There are many other aspects of these and other Bible characters of which you will want to make note in your workbook.

In regards to a better understanding of Christ and the Church in the New Testament, make a special study of the following items of this period:

Genesis 12:1-3: The Abrahamic Covenant. Study Galatians 3 along with this.

Genesis 14:18-19: After reading about Melchizedek here, read also Hebrews 5, 6 and 7.

Genesis 16: Read how the Bible interprets this chapter in Galatians 4.

Genesis 28:11-12: There is a parallel of this dream of Jacob's in John 1:51.

Genesis 49:9-10: Leading up to this prophecy, we have the following:

The promise of a redeemer, Genesis 3:15;

Seth, son of Adam and Eve, head of the Messianic line;

Abraham, head of the Messianic nation;

Isaac heir to the promise given to Abraham;

Jacob, father of the twelve tribes of Israel;

Judah, the Messianic tribe.

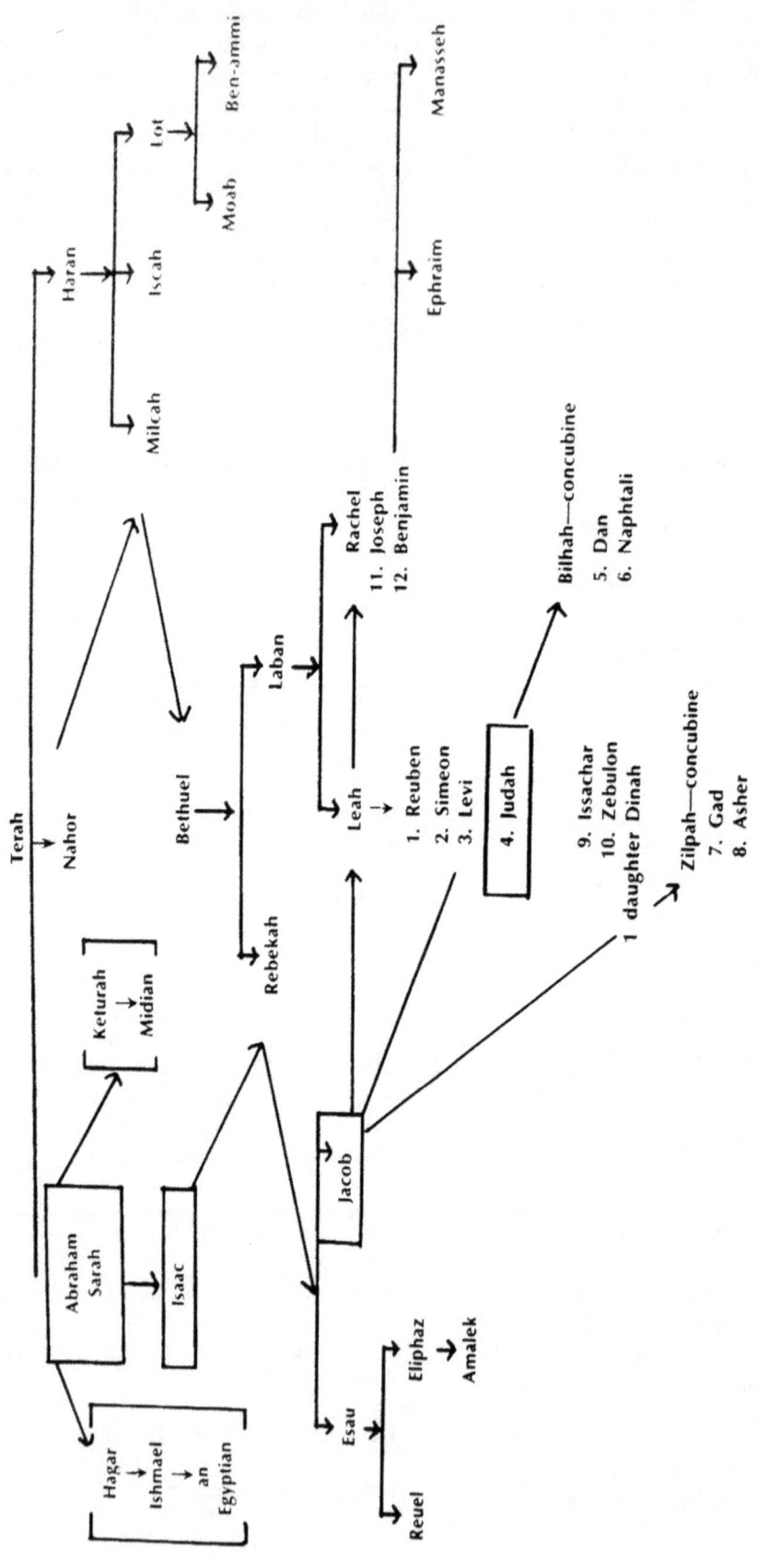

With the chart on the opposite page in front of you, notice the interrelationship of the family of **Terah**.

Terah had three sons, Abraham, Nahor and Haran, Genesis 11:27.

Abraham's wife was **Sarah**, verse 29, who was also his half-sister, Genesis 20:12.

Haran had one son, **Lot**, and two daughters, **Milcah and Iscah**, Genesis 11:27, 29.

Nahor married his niece, Milcah, Genesis 11:29. They had eight sons, one of whom was Bethuel, Genesis 22:22. Bethuel had a daughter, Rebekah, verse 23, and a son, Laban, Genesis 24:29.

Abraham and Sarah had a son, **Isaac**, Genesis 21:3.

Isaac married Rebekah, Genesis 24, and they had twin boys, Esau and Jacob, Genesis 25:21-26.

Laban had two daughters, **Leah and Rachel**, Genesis 29.

Jacob married Leah and Rachel, Genesis 29.

Jacob and Leah had six sons, **Reuben, Simeon, Levi, Judah, Issachar and Zebulon**, Genesis 29:32-35; 30:17-20; also one daughter, Dinah, verse 21. By Zilpah, Leah's hand-maiden, Jacob had two sons, Gad and Asher, Genesis 30:9-13.

Jacob and Rachel had two sons, **Joseph and Benjamin,** Genesis 30:22-24; 35:16-18. By Bilhah, Rachel's handmaiden, Jacob had two sons, Dan and Naphtali, Genesis 30:3-8.

These twelve boys become the heads of the twelve tribes of Israel: Israel was Jacob's name, Genesis 32:28.

Abraham also had a son, **Ishmael**, by Hagar, Sarah's handmaiden. Ishmael married an Egyptian woman, Genesis 21:21, from whom come the Ishmaelites.

Esau, whose name is also Edam, Genesis 25:30, married one of the daughters of Ishmael, by whom he had a son, Reuel, Genesis 36:4. He also married a Hittite woman, verse 2, by whom he has a son, Eliphaz, verse 4. Eliphaz had a son, Amalek, verse 12, from whom the Amalekites come.

Lot, son of Haran, had married and had two daughters, Genesis 19. After the death of his wife, verse 26, Lot had two sons by his two daughters, verses 31-38. Their names were Moab and Ben-ammi, from whom the Moabites and Ammonites come, verses 37-38.

After the death of Sarah, Abraham married Keturah, Genesis 25:1. They had six sons, verse 2, one of whom was Midian. It was to the land of Midian that Moses fled from Egypt, Exodus 2:15.

Also notice that Joseph had two sons, **Ephraim and Manasseh**, Genesis 41:51-52. These two sons received Joseph's inheritance in the **Promised Land**, see map at 6 o'clock.

Now, since Moses fled to the **Midianites** at the beginning of 4 o'clock; the new nation of Israel contend with the Amalekites coming out of Egypt at 4 o'clock; the Israelites are refused passage through the land of the Edomites in the last year of the wanderings at 5 o'clock; they also contend with the **Moabites and Ammonites** in that last year at 5 o'clock, I thought it would be well to point out the relationship of these people. The fact that God took special care of the descendants of Abraham, Isaac and Jacob caused much envy and strife with the descendants of Lot, Ishmael and Esau. Throughout the national life of Israel the battles were frequent with these people.

We have already noticed, at 2 o'clock, from whom the **Egyptians and Canaanites** descend.

- STUDY NOTES -

- STUDY NOTES -

- STUDY NOTES -

VI. 4 o'clock
EGYPTIAN BONDAGE EXODUS

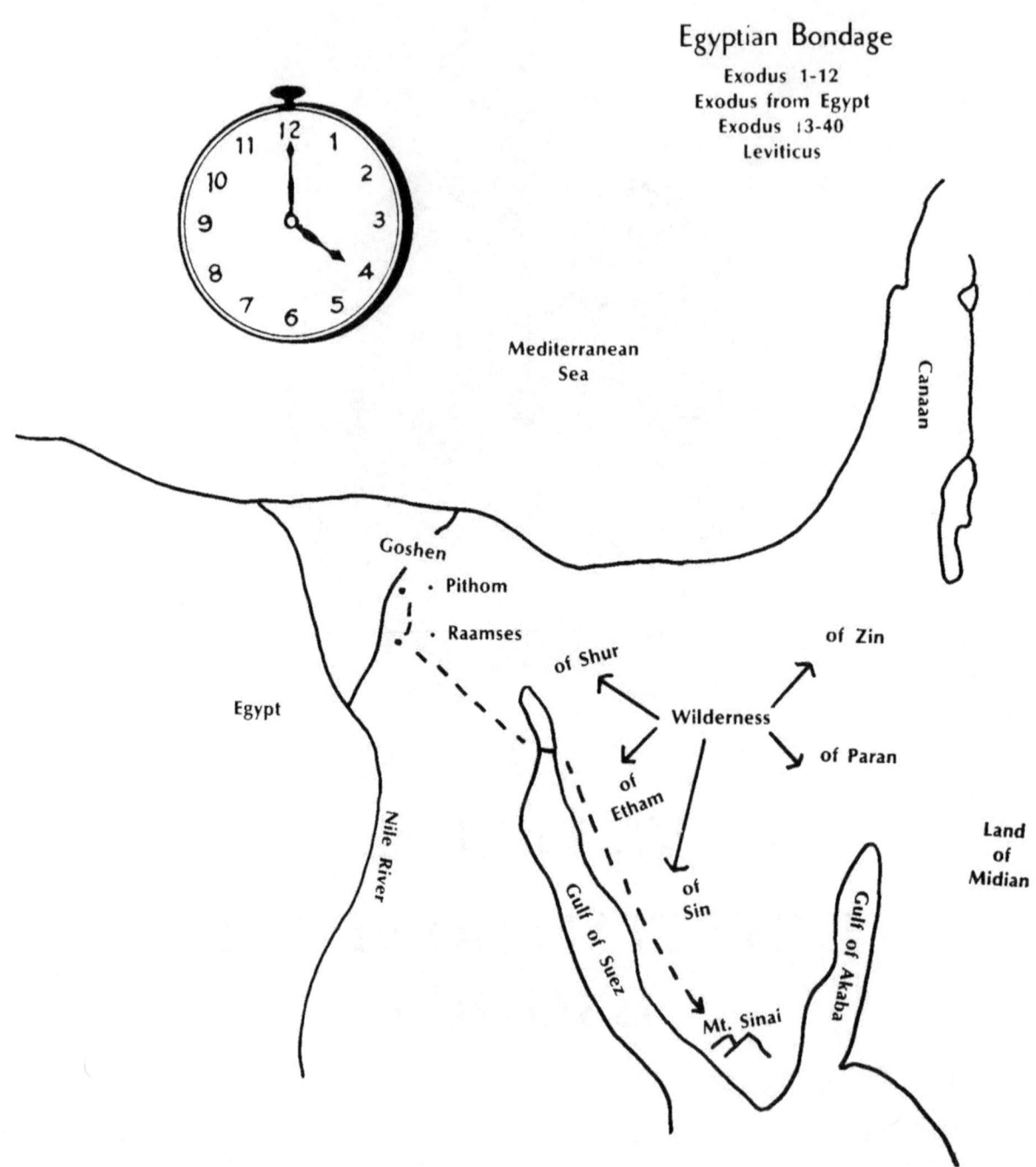

Geography

As the map shows, the book of Exodus contains the bondage in Egypt, the journey to **Mt. Sinai** and those activities of the year spent at Mt. Sinai.

Goshen is that portion of land given, by Pharaoh, to the family of Joseph.

Pithom and **Raamses** are the two storehouse cities that the Israelites were forced to build under bondage.

If it were not for the **Nile River** and its seasonal overflow, Egypt would not be inhabitable. Therefore Egypt is called "the gift of the Nile."

The **Gulf of Suez**, the west arm of the **Red Sea**, is about 200 miles long. The **Gulf of Akaba**, the east arm of the Red Sea, is about 100 miles long. The main body of the Red Sea flows south and east, until it empties into the Indian Ocean, as does the Persian Gulf.

The Israelites crossed over into the wilderness of **Shur** and traveled down the east side of the Gulf of Suez, through the wilderness of Sin, to **Mt. Sinai**.

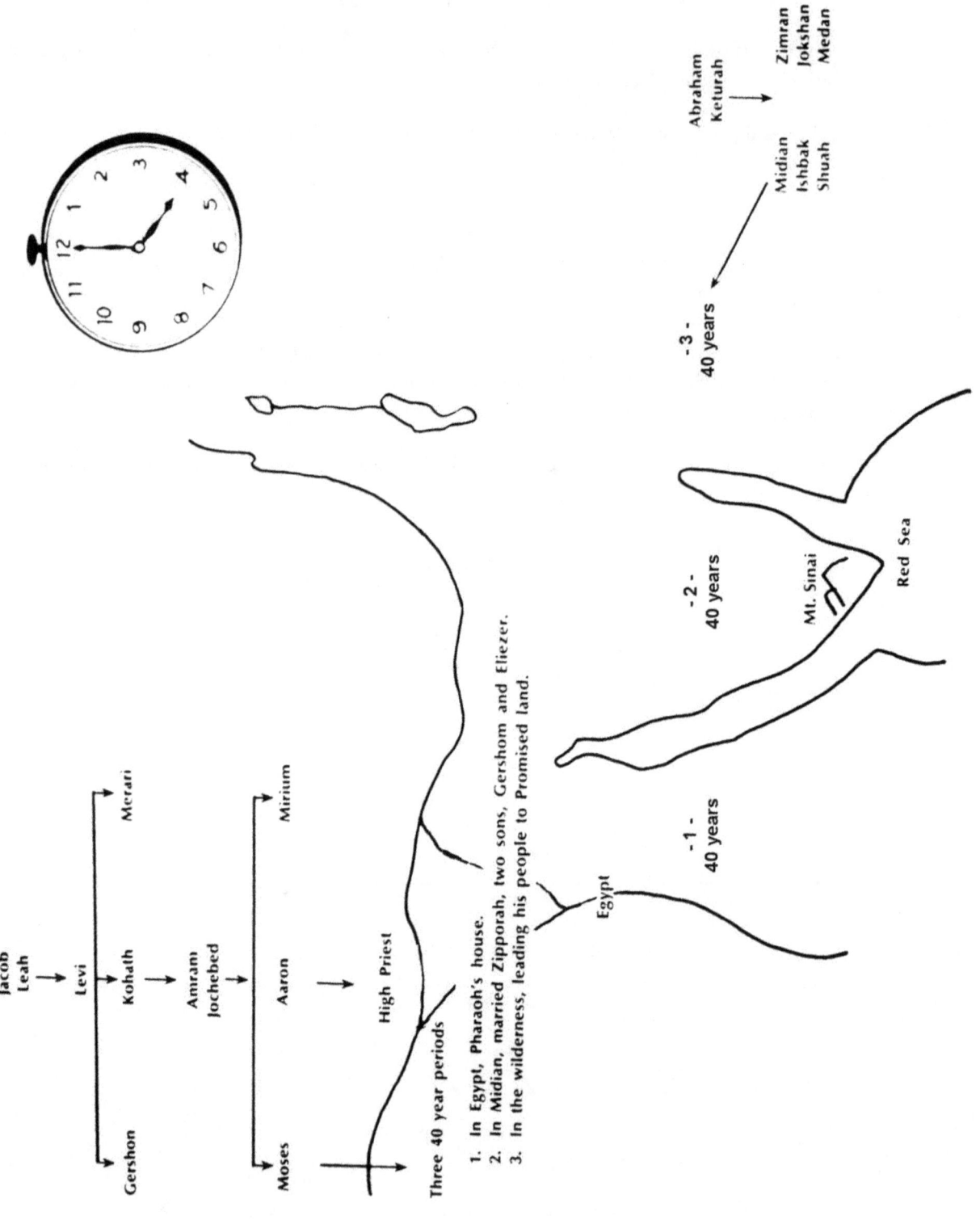

Egyptian Bondage

Exodus 1-12; 13-40
Leviticus

We have no way of knowing how long it was after Joseph's death that the conditions arose under which **Moses** was born. It is suggested that at the time of Joseph there were men ruling Egypt who were not of Egyptian birth. These outsiders would be easily drawn to other strangers such as Joseph and his family. Then by the time of Moses the **Egyptians** had regained control of their country. This would explain the apprehension of the rapid growth of the Israelites. Their concern was that the Israelites could usurp the throne of Egypt or assist an outside source, Exodus 1:10. This explains their putting the Israelites under bondage and attempting to stop their growth by slaying all the Hebrew baby boys as they are born.

God, of course, has other plans for His people. **Egypt serves as an incubator** for the purpose of allowing this small family to grow into a great nation of people, this in fulfillment of God's promise to Abraham.

The book of Exodus opens with the people under bondage and the slaying of the Hebrew babies. **Moses is born at this time.** Notice that he is a descendent of Levi, third son of Jacob by Leah. The life of Moses can be arranged into three 40 year periods. The first 40 years was spent in the house of Pharaoh as the son of Pharaoh's daughter, Exodus 2:1-10. As you can see, the Bible is very brief on this first 40 years. The second 40 years is spent in the land of Midian, Exodus 2:11-4:28. Moses works for a man named **Jethro**, or as his name is in Exodus 2:18, Reuel. He married Zipporah, one of the seven daughters of Jethro. It was at the close of this second period of Moses' life that God appeared to him in the flame of the **burning bush** while tending the flock of Jethro on **Mt. Horeb, or as better known, Mt. Sinai**, Exodus 3:1. He and his brother Aaron are sent to Egypt to lead the people of Israel out of bondage, in answer to their cry to God, Exodus 2:23-25; 4:27-31. **The last 40 years of Moses' life is spent in accomplishing this great task.**

The activities of this last phase of Moses' life are as full of detail as the other two are lacking in detail. It requires the reading of the remaining thirty-six chapters of **Exodus** and all of the books of **Numbers** and **Deuteronomy** for these details, some of which are of great importance to the understanding of a large portion of the New Testament concerning Christ and His Church.

In Exodus 1-12 we find the children of Israel in bondage in Egypt. Exodus 13-40 tells of **the journey from Egypt to Mt. Sinai**. So it is within the first twelve chapters that the ten plagues take place. The first one takes place in Exodus 7 and the last one in Exodus 12. You will, of course, want to make your own notes on these plagues out of your Bible.

In Exodus 13-40 you will want to take special notice of the tabernacle and its furnishings with their varied functions. The writer of the book of Hebrews, in the New Testament, makes great use of the book of Exodus. With a thorough study of the **tabernacle** and **priesthood** at this time, we are better prepared for the understanding of the New Testament. The goal of this study of the Old Testament is a better understanding of the New Testament.

In Exodus 13 the people go across the west arm of the **Red Sea, also known as the Gulf of Suez.** They arrive at Sinai in Exodus 19:1. **I find it easier to remember where to return for a certain study if I mark the activities into certain chapters.** So from Exodus 13-19 we have the three month journey from Egypt to Sinai, some 200 miles. Within these chapters we read of God's great care over His people. The **manna** was sent down from heaven for use as directed, Exodus 16:4-5. This manna sustained the people throughout the 40 years in the wilderness and ceased as they ate of **the fruit of the land of Canaan**, Joshua 5:12. Jesus applies the idea of the true manna to Himself in John 6. It is always good to add these New Testament notations to your notes of the immediate study for a more gradual understanding of how the Old Testament relates to the New Testament.]

Twice in the wilderness God sends **quail** down when the people complain about the lack of meat, Exodus 16:13 and Numbers 11:31-34. When there is no **water**, God provides, Exodus 17:1-6. In the other instance of bringing water from the rock, Moses acts in such a way as to void his chance of entering the Promised Land, Numbers 20. Moses said the second time, **"Must we fetch you water out of this rock."** God explains the wrong in this in verse 12.

Israel fights its first battle after leaving Egypt, Exodus 17. It is with **the Amalekites, the descendants of Esau.** Amalek was Esau's grandson, Genesis 36:12. They lived in the northern part of the Sinai Peninsula around Kadesh-barnea, of which we will learn more at 5 o'clock. The Israelites were victorious in this first battle, verses 8-16, but those who fought the Amalekites at 5 o'clock were not so successful because God was not with them in that second battle, Numbers 14.

When Moses left Midian to go to Egypt, he left his wife and two sons in Midian with Jethro. We find Jethro bringing **Zipporah** and the two boys to Moses in the wilderness. Here both boys are named, Exodus 18:1-4; in Exodus 2:22 only one boy, Gershom, is mentioned. **Moses' two sons are Gershom and Eliezer.**

In Exodus 19 the Israelites arrive at Mt. Sinai, where the remaining activities of the book of Exodus occur. **They stay at Mt. Sinai for one year and one month,** Numbers 10:11. During this time the tabernacle is built. The instructions are given in Exodus 25-31. God gives certain and specific instructions as to every detail. In Exodus 35-40 we find these instructions repeated as the tabernacle is built to these certain and specific details. God is never evasive about His instructions. We need only to study His word to know what His will is, 2 Timothy 2:15.

In Exodus 20 the Ten Commandments are listed. When Moses goes up into the mountain to receive **the law written on tables of stone**, along with **instructions for the tabernacle and the priesthood**, Aaron leads the people in the building of the **golden calf**. Read this and remember it, because at 9 o'clock, as the kingdom divides, we find Jeroboam building two of these calves. He had spent some time in Egypt before he was made king of the northern kingdom of Israel. More about this at 9 o'clock.

When Moses saw the people reveling in their idolatry he was so angry that he broke the tables of stone. Read how Aaron tries to blame the whole thing on the people, Exodus 32:21-24. Compare his story with what actually happened, verses 1-6.

In Exodus 34 Moses is instructed to make two tables of stone like the first and bring them with him into the mountain and there God rewrites the ten commandments upon the stones, verse 28. He is in the mountain for another 40 days, but this time the people have managed to behave themselves and wait for his return.

The tabernacle is started and the people are so willing to bring all they have toward the building of it that Moses finally has to tell them to stop, Exodus 36:1-6. The details of the tabernacle is a study all its own, so you will want to remember where to return to make that detailed study.

For an outline of the study of this most interesting book you might consider the following chapters division:

Exodus 1-12: The Israelites under Egyptian bondage.

Exodus 13-19: The journey from Egypt to Mt. Sinai.

Exodus 20-24: The Ten Commandments given, among other laws and ordinances.

Exodus 25-31: The instructions for the building of the tabernacle; also laws concerning the priesthood.

Exodus 32-34: Aaron leads the people in the building of the golden calf. Moses returns to the mountain for the second 40 days as God rewrites the Ten Commandments.

Exodus 35-40: The tabernacle is built.

The book of **Leviticus** is so named because it contains that system of laws which were to be administered by the priests. God had set aside the entire tribe of Levi for this purpose. There were additional laws given during the wilderness wanderings, but for the most part they are recorded in the book of Leviticus. **These laws, of both spiritual and social nature, were given during that year at Mt. Sinai, and in preparation for life in the Promised Land.**

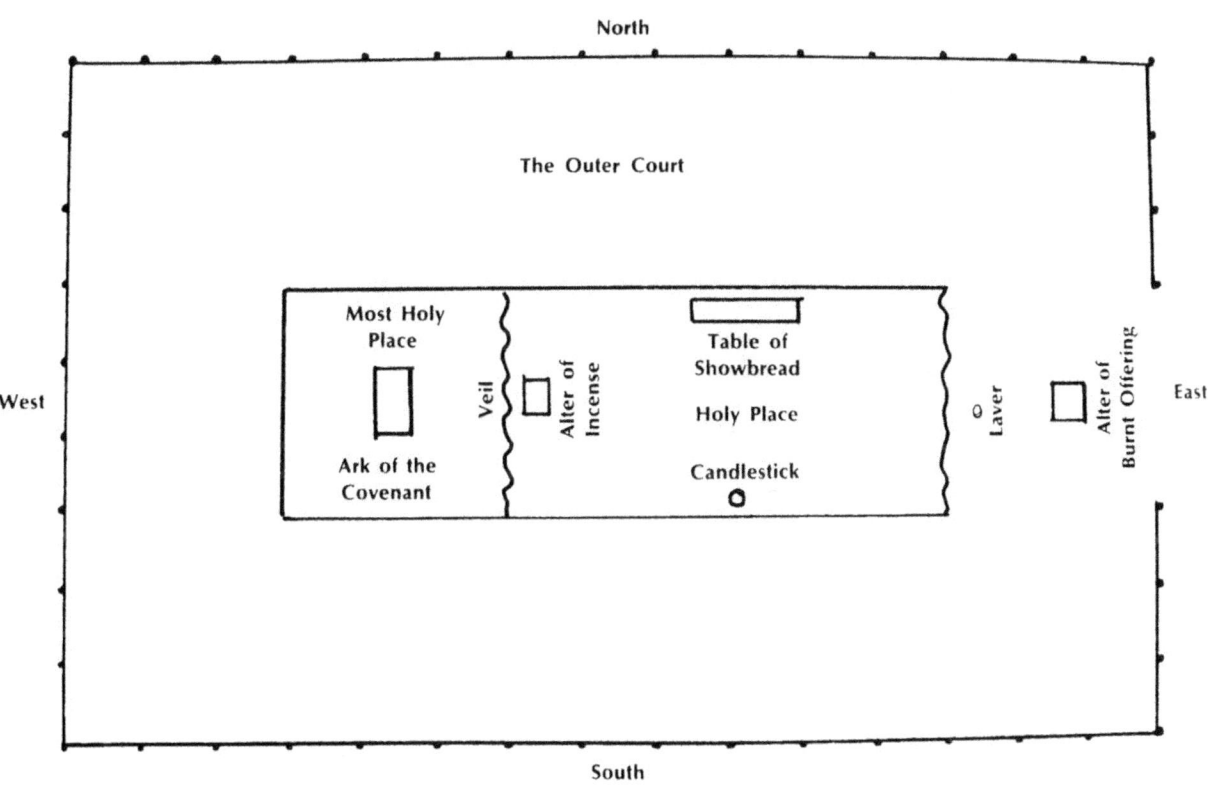

- STUDY NOTES -

- STUDY NOTES -

STUDY NOTES

VII. 5 o'clock
WILDERNESS WANDERINGS

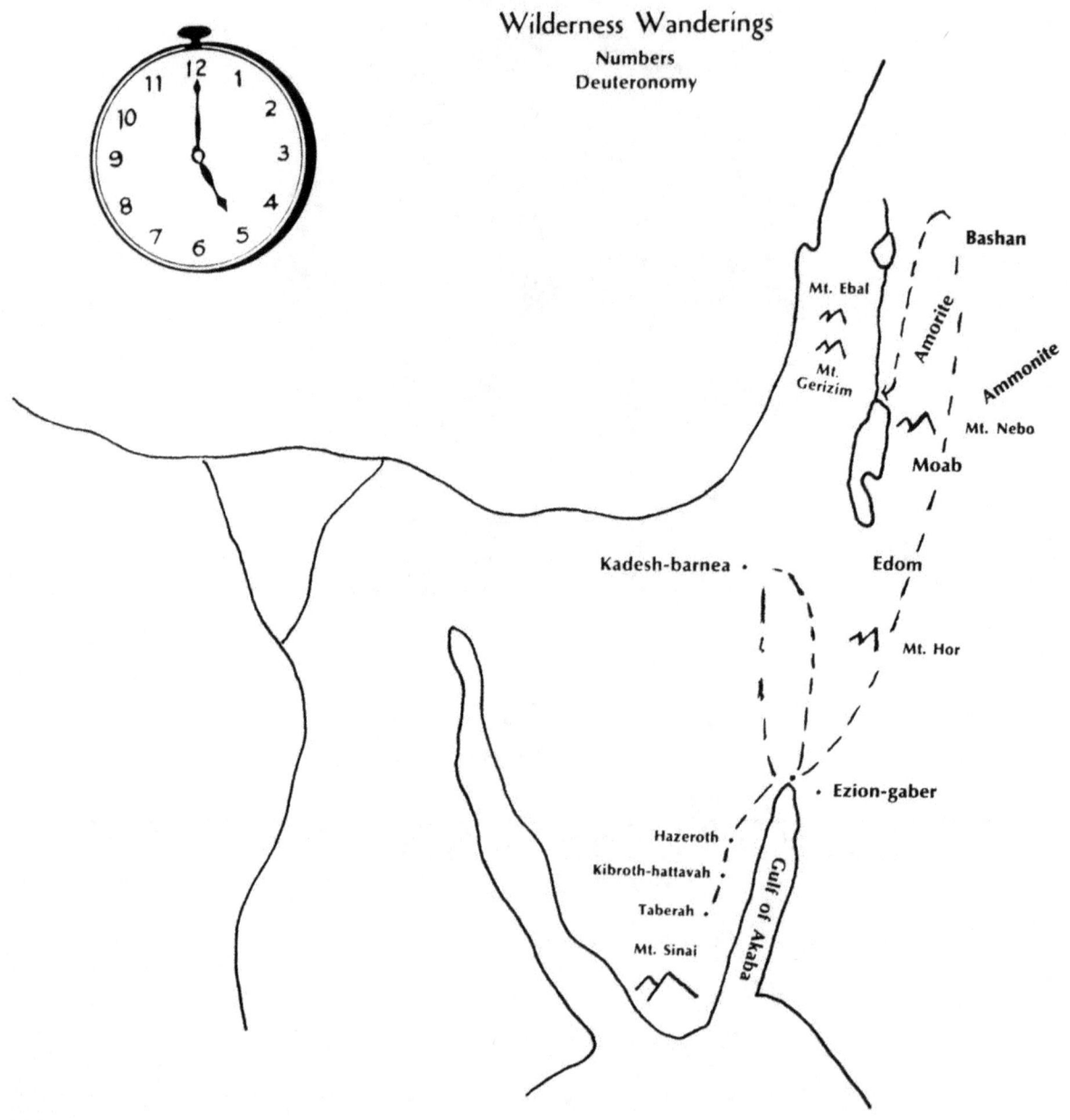

Geography

As 5 o'clock opens we find the people still gathered around **Mt. Sinai**. Preparations are being made for the journey to Canaan.

As they leave, they travel up the western side of the east arm of the Red Sea, the **Gulf of Akaba**.

Taberah was so named because God caused a fire to burn the people because of their complaining.

Kibroth-hattavah was so named because of a plague God sent among the people because of their greed.

Hazeroth was where Aaron and Miriam became jealous of Moses, and Miriam was struck with leprosy.

Kadesh-barnea was where the people were encamped when God told Moses to send the spies into the land of Canaan.

Mt. Hor was where Aaron died the last year of the wanderings.

They traveled around **Edom**, up through **Moab** and conquered the countries of the **Amorite** and **Bashan** on the eastern side of the Jordan River.

Mt. Nebo was where Moses died.

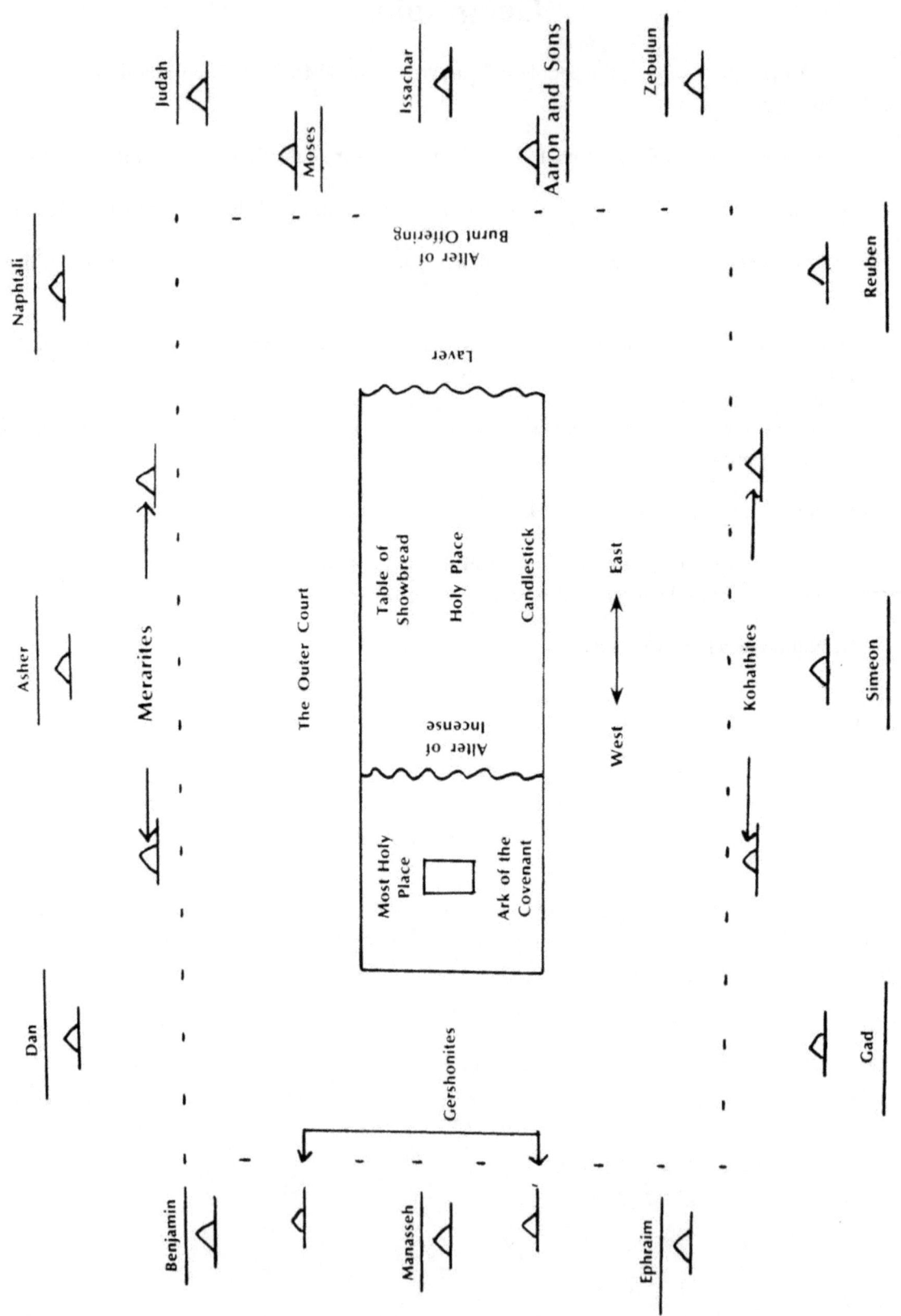

Wilderness Wanderings

Numbers
Deuteronomy
Sinai to Canaan

There is no transition to be made from 4 o'clock to 5 o'clock, because **Numbers begins where Exodus leaves off**. Not so with Genesis and Exodus.

The Israelites are still at Mt. Sinai. In the first nine chapters preparations are underway for the journey to the land of **Canaan,** or "Promised Land." The **tabernacle** has been built, the priesthood has been instituted with Aaron and his sons as high priests, and the tribe of Levi set apart to assist in the functioning of the tabernacle. Certain and specific laws have been given for both the spiritual and social lives of the people. A new nation is born and its governing laws have been given; now all the people have to do is go up, and with God's help, take the land He promised to Abraham and his seed.

In prospect of fighting the battles of the conquest, there is a numbering of the men 20 years and older, men able to go to war, Numbers 1:2-3, the total of which is 603,550, verse 46. Notice this number and we will compare it to the second numbering at the end of the 40 years of wandering in the wilderness. **This book derives its name from these two numberings of the army of Israel.**

Numbers 2 shows how **the tabernacle is to be the very center of the life of Israel.** On the opposite page you will see this graphically illustrated. The tabernacle was always set up in the center of the encampment as they traveled from place to place. It was always to face the east. The tribes were to encamp on all four sides of the tabernacle:

Judah, Issachar and Zebulon on the east; Dan, Asher and Naphtali on the north; Benjamin, Manasseh and Ephraim on the west; Gad, Simeon and Reuben on the south.

Numbers 3 tells how the Levites were to settle on all four sides and the reason is given in Numbers 1:53.

Moses, Aaron and Aaron's sons on the east;

the **Merarites** on the north;

the **Gershonites** on the west;

the **Kohathites** on the south.

Remember that **Merari, Gershon and Kohath were the sons of Levi**, Exodus 6:16, and that Moses and Aaron were the grandsons of Kohath, Exodus 6:18, 20.

Only the Levites were to care for the tabernacle and all things pertaining to it, Numbers 3. God was very explicit in this. At 8 o'clock we have one well-meaning young man who forgot this for a moment and it cost him his life, 2 Samuel 6:3-7. Also, only those males between the ages of 30 and 50 were to enter the service of the tabernacle, Numbers 4.

From Numbers 5 through Numbers 8 numerous laws are given, among which are those of offering sacrifices, and in Exodus 9 **the people observe the first Passover feast.** This feast was instituted for the purpose of remembering how God delivered His people out of Egyptian bondage with the last of the ten plagues.

In Numbers 10-12 the people journey from Mt. Sinai to Kadesh-barnea, in the wilderness of Paran. They travel up the west side of the Gulf of Akaba, the east arm of the Red Sea. It was a straight course up to the land of Canaan. They could have accomplished it in a short time. However, we see them turned back because of their **lack of faith** in the promise of God. In Numbers 11 the people complain the second time of the lack of meat to eat. God sends the quail, but along with the quail He sends a plague, verses 18-35. In Numbers 12 Miriam and Aaron complain about Moses, and **Miriam is stricken with leprosy.**

From Kadesh-barnea **twelve men, one from each tribe, were sent in to spy out the land of Canaan**, Numbers 13:1-25. Among the twelve was the young man, Joshua, who led in that first battle out of Egypt with the Amalekites at 4 o'clock, Exodus 17:8-16. Of the twelve men who were sent into Canaan, **only Joshua and a young man named Caleb remained faithful to the promise of God** that the land was theirs for the taking. The other ten gave an unfavorable report and the people refuse to go in and take the land. Because of their lack of faith in Him, God sentences the people to wander in the wilderness one year for every day the spies spent in Canaan, which were forty days. Also, of those who refused to go up and take the land, all those 20 years and older, would die in the wilderness, never to see the Promised Land, Numbers 14:20-29. Some of the people then try to go up into the land. They are met by the Amalekites the second time, but this time they are utterly defeated, verses 40-45.

Some laws concerning offerings are in Numbers 15. In Exodus 16 there is **the rebellion led by Korah**, of the tribe of Levi, verse 1. Since he was of the priestly tribe we see that he is questioning Aaron's authority among the priests. In Exodus 17 God makes it very clear who has authority by **the budding of Aaron's rod**. In Numbers 18 we see how the Levites are to receive their inheritance. Various laws of purification are given in Numbers 19.

Then between the 19th chapter and the 20th chapter, 38 years have gone by. We notice in Numbers 10:11 that the people left Mt. Sinai in the second year, the second month and the twentieth day after the exodus from Egypt. They journey to **Kadesh-barnea** from where the spies are sent. Then the activities of Numbers 15-19 seem to be things which needed to be settled early; **the authority of Moses and of Aaron; feast days and such laws concerning the worship.** Then in Numbers 20:28 we have the death of Aaron on Mt. Hor, which Numbers 33:38 says happened in the fortieth year out of Egypt. So in chapters 20 through 36 we have the last year of the wanderings.

In Numbers 20 we also have the second time God brings **water out of the rock**; the first being at 4 o'clock, Exodus 17:1-6. Moses apparently takes the credit for bringing the water forth this time, verse 10, for which God deprives him of bringing Israel into the Promised Land, verse 12.

Also in Numbers 20 we meet the **Edomites, descendants of Esau**, Genesis 25:30. The land of Edom is at the lower end of the Dead Sea. The Edomites refuse to let the Israelites pass through their land, verses 14-21. They then turn south to Mt. Hor where Aaron dies, verse 28. They travel down to the tip of the **Gulf of Akaba** in order to go around Edom, Numbers 21:4. The people murmur because of the manna and the lack of water, and God sends the serpents among them, Numbers 21:5-9. [After reading about the **brazen serpent** here, turn to John 3:14-15 and read how Jesus applies this to Himself.] The people made an idol of the brazen serpent, and Hezekiah destroyed it at 10 o'clock, 2 Kings 18:4.

They journey north toward the country of Moab, just skirting the country of Ammon. They travel through the country of Gilead, all the way up to Bashan on the east of the Sea of Galilee, Numbers 22-25. Notice in Numbers 22, the Midianites, among whom Moses lived for 40 years, conspire with the Moabites against the Israelites. It is with Balaam, the soothsayer, that **Balak, king of Moab**, conspires to curse the Israelites. God, however, causes Balaam to bless the Israelites each time they are supposed to be cursed, Numbers 22-24. This is one of the most memorable stories of this 5 o'clock period.

The people arrive in the plains east of the Jordan River. **The second census is taken**, Numbers 26. Remember when they were numbered in the first chapter, at Sinai, the number was 603,550, Numbers 1:46. Now, after 38 years of wandering and the death of all those 20 years and older, the number is still 601,730, verse 51. Remember, too, that the numberings are of the men 20 years and older, able to go to war, Numbers 26:2; excluding the Levites: in other words, the army.

In Numbers 27 Joshua is chosen to lead the people into the Promised Land. In the remaining chapters of this book various laws are given. **Reuben, Gad and Manasseh are given inheritance on the east of the Jordan**, but Moses warns them that their men need to plan to go into the land of Canaan to help fight the battles of the conquest, Numbers 32:6-11. Forty-eight cities throughout the land are designated for the Levites, Numbers 35, and of these, six are cities of refuge; three on the east of the Jordan and three on the west, verses 13-34.

To outline the study of this book, the chapter division would be the following:

Chapters

Numbers 1-10:11: Last days at Mt. Sinai.

Numbers 11-14: The journey from Sinai to Kadesh-barnea.

Numbers 15-19: All that is recorded of 38 years of the wanderings.

Numbers 20-36: The last year of the wanderings.

Remember that this is the third and last period of Moses' life. The book of Deuteronomy records the last days of his life.

Deuteronomy

It has been said, "If a nation will not learn of its history, it is bound to repeat it."

In essence this is what the book of Deuteronomy is all about. **Deuteronomy means "the law repeated."** The book contains three addresses to the people by **Moses**. The people are gathered there on the east of the Jordan River, ready to go in and conquer the land promised to Abraham and his descendants by God. What God is really trying to do, through Moses, is have the people look back at their history for the past 40 years so that they will be better prepared for life in the Promised Land. Remember that because of the unbelief on the part of the people in Numbers 13-14, there is a new generation of people gathered together. Of the first numbering of the army, 603,550, only Joshua and Caleb are alive, Numbers 32:11-12.

Moses' **first address** begins in Deuteronomy 1:6. He begins his speech by going back to their stay at Mt. Sinai. He reminds them of God's promise to Abraham, Isaac and Jacob; the promise of a great nation of people, Deuteronomy 1:10 and a land prepared for their possession, verse 8. He reminds them of the journey from Mt. Horeb, or Sinai, to Kadesh-barnea, where that generation refused to go in and possess the land; for which many died in the wilderness, Deuteronomy 1:23-46.

Then Moses seems to skip over thirty-eight years and turns his attention to the last year and the journey from Kadesh-barnea to Edam, through Moab, up to Bashan and back down to the plains of Moab, Deuteronomy 2-3.

In Deuteronomy 4:1-40 Moses calls for more strict obedience to God's commands, especially concerning **idolatry**, which we will find is their major problem throughout the years from the period of the Judges to the Captivity. So we see that the first address of Moses is in Deuteronomy 1:6 to 4:40.

He then takes the time to designate those three cities of refuge on the east of the Jordan, among the tribes of Reuben and Gad and the half tribe of Manasseh. These three cities were **Bezer** in the tribe of Reuben; **Ramoth** in Gad and **Golan** in Manasseh, Deuteronomy 4:41-43.

In Deuteronomy 5 Moses begins his **second address** to the people. He repeats the Ten Commandments, so we see that the Ten Commandments are in Exodus 20 and Deuteronomy 5. He makes a statement in Deuteronomy 5:2-3 which is important to remember when you are discussing the Law of Moses and for whom it was given.

In Deuteronomy 6 it is interesting to note two of the three statements **Jesus** made to the devil during the temptation in Matthew 4:10 and Luke 4:8. Read Matthew and Luke and see how He uses verses 13 and 16 of this chapter. Then turn to Deuteronomy 8:3 for the third statement Jesus made to the devil. Also notice in Deuteronomy 6:5 a statement Jesus used when asked which was the greatest commandment of the law in Matthew 22:36-37.

Deuteronomy 6-8 are thrilling chapters. Be sure to not deprive yourself of the reading of the text itself.

Moses reminds the people of the building of the **golden calf at Mt. Sinai**. They were so frightened they wanted Moses to go up to receive the law, Deuteronomy 9-10. Then he goes all the way back to the crossing of the Red Sea, coming out of Egypt, and the destruction of Pharaoh's army: also Korah's rebellion and its consequences. His **exhortation** is that they should remember how God is with them when they are obedient, and that they should keep His commandments in order to live long and happy lives in the land He has prepared for them, Deuteronomy 11.

In Deuteronomy 12 the people are told they should utterly destroy any and all **idols** they encounter as they go through the land, and that even they will not be offering **sacrifices** just anywhere; there will be specific times and places for these sacrifices. They are forbidden to eat the blood of the animal; they are to pour it out as they would water on the ground.

There are good prophets and bad prophets: good dreamers and bad dreamers, and the way you can tell the difference is the direction they want to lead you, Deuteronomy 13. Even if it is your mate, son or daughter, who tries to lead you away from worshipping God, stoning is to be the sentence, verses 6-10.

The **clean and unclean animals** are described in Deuteronomy 14. There was slavery, even among the Hebrews, Deuteronomy 15:12, and every seven years the bondman was to be released if he desired to leave. The reading of Deuteronomy 16 will help us to remember the three most solemn feasts of the year and what prompted their observance.

The Passover: in remembrance of their deliverance from Egyptian Bondage; to be kept at a certain place, Deuteronomy 16:6.

The Feast of Weeks: offering of the first fruits of their labor, remembering the bountiful land God had given them, Deuteronomy 16:4-12.

The Feast of Tabernacles: in remembrance of the wandering in the wilderness.

In Deuteronomy 17 Moses says to take any hard matter to the Levites and judges to be settled. Moses looks toward the time that the people will be asking for a king to rule over them and mentions the grave responsibility these kings will have toward the Word of God, verses 14-20. You will find that not one king of the United Kingdom at 8 o'clock or the Divided Kingdom at 9 o'clock or Judah Alone at 10 o'clock really measured up. Read verse 17 and think of Solomon. The fact is, they either forgot what God said, verses 14-20, or, as in the case of the kings of the northern kingdom of Israel at 9 o'clock, they made no pretense of interest in acknowledging God in any way. **Very few, four out of twenty, of the kings of David's line, the southern kingdom of Judah, attempted to know God and His will.**

The Levites are to receive their inheritance from among the people they serve, Deuteronomy 18:1-7. Does this remind you of what Paul said in 1 Corinthians 9:14? I am sure it applies. Also in Deuteronomy 18 we have the prophecy of the Divine Prophet, verses 15, 18; a prophecy of Christ.

In Deuteronomy 19 we have an explanation of the situation in which a man would need to go to a city of refuge; also the punishment of a **false witness** and the need for more than one witness.

No matter what the outlook is, as far as the people of Canaan are concerned, the people are to take heart; **God is with them**, Deuteronomy 20. A stubborn son is to be dealt with, Deuteronomy 21:18-21. If you are the mother of a son, aren't you thankful to live under the law of Christ instead of the Law of Moses?

Laws of humanity are dealt with in Deuteronomy 22; the distinguishing of the sexes by apparel, verse 5; of harlotry, verses 13-21; of adultery, verse 22; of rape, verses 23-27; of fornication, verses 28-29 and of incest, verse 30. Those who are allowed to enter the congregation of the Lord is explained in Deuteronomy 23. That **bill of divorcement** that Jesus spoke about in Matthew 19 is given in Deuteronomy 24. The way Miriam was dealt with because of her leprosy, Numbers 12, establishes the laws concerning the **leper** in Deuteronomy 24:8-9. Deuteronomy 25:1-3 establishes the law that a man could not be beaten with more than forty stripes. Paul said he was beaten with forty stripes save one, 2 Corinthians 11:24. The reading of Deuteronomy 25:5-10 will help to explain what Boaz attends to in obtaining Ruth for his wife, Ruth 4, at 7:30 o'clock.

With Deuteronomy 26 the second address of Moses ends, being the longest of the three addresses, Deuteronomy 5-26.

From Mt. Ebal and Mt. Gerizim, in Canaan, the **blessings and cursings** are to be read: the blessings from Mt. Gerizim, Deuteronomy 27:12; the cursing from Mt. Ebal, Deuteronomy 27:13-26. Both blessings and cursings are listed in Deuteronomy 28. Notice the warning in Deuteronomy 28:60 and compare it with the alternative in Deuteronomy 7:15. Their clothes did not wear out in the wilderness, Deuteronomy 29.5, 8.4.

God promises to have **compassion** for them when they turn to Him, Deuteronomy 30. We find Him doing this over and over during the period of the Judges at 7 o'clock. They follow God as long as their leader does. When there was no leader, they were like lost sheep. However, each time they cry to God He has compassion for them and raises another leader. Deuteronomy 30 ends the third address of Moses: Deuteronomy 27-30.

Beginning in Deuteronomy 31 Moses is no longer speaking in retrospect. He speaks for the moment and the future. He is both optimistic and pessimistic. With some words he encourages the people and yet he tells them of their future apostasy.

God tells Moses that the time has come that he will die, Deuteronomy 31:16. Moses, himself, says he is 120 years of age, verse 2. God gives the charge of the people to Joshua, verse 23. The **song of Moses** is recorded in Deuteronomy 32:1-43. Then God directs Moses to go up to Mt. Nebo, but before he goes he blesses the tribes, Deuteronomy 33. Moses goes up to **Mt. Nebo, also called Pisgah,** Deuteronomy 34:1. God shows him the land of promise; he then dies, verse 5, and God buries him, verse 6. Notice Moses' physical condition at the time of his death, verse 7. There were thirty days of mourning for Moses. Joshua takes on the spirit and wisdom of Moses, and the people listen to him as they did Moses.

Although Deuteronomy is a retelling of the activities of Exodus and Numbers, Deuteronomy adds the last few days of Moses' life and the account of his death.

To remember more closely where certain things are located in Deuteronomy, I divide the book according to the three addresses of Moses:

First Address: Deuteronomy 1:6-4:40

Second Address: Deuteronomy 5-26

Third Address: Deuteronomy 27-30

Last days and death of Moses on Mt. Nebo: Deuteronomy 31-34

- STUDY NOTES -

- STUDY NOTES -

- STUDY NOTES -

VIII. 6 o'clock
CONQUEST

Conquest of Canaan
Joshua

The six cities of refuge are underlined.
Shiloh and Gilgal were religious headquarters.

Canaan Divided Among the Twelve Tribes

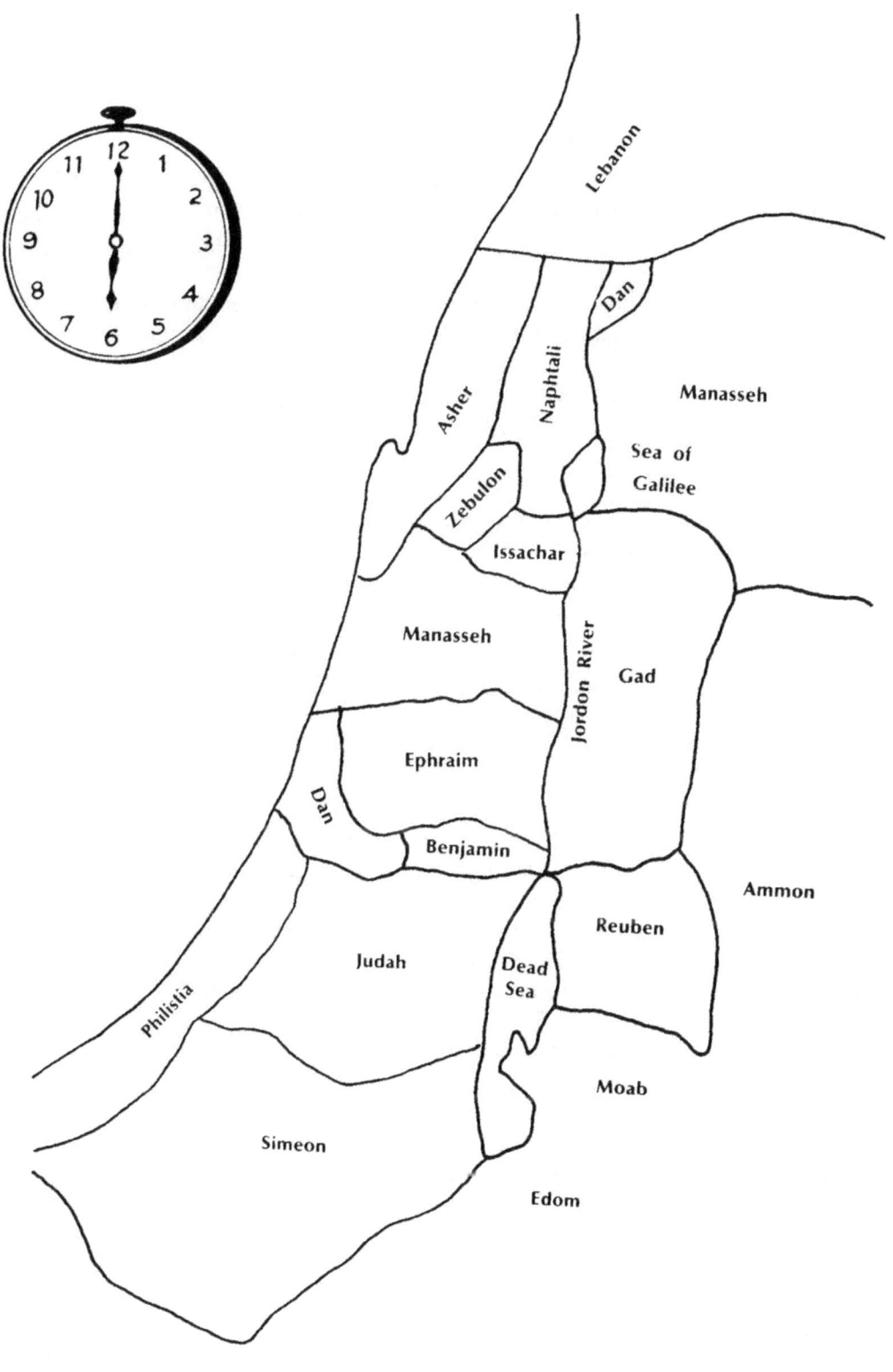

Geography

On the first map for this 6 o'clock period there are some of the cities the Israelites captured as they went into Canaan. Many of these cities are city kingdoms. Remember that Abraham paid tithes to **Melchizedek, king of Salem**. So as we go into the book of Joshua we will meet other kings of other cities.

It should be brought out that the city of **Jerusalem** was not so called until 8 o'clock when David captures the city and it becomes the civil and religious headquarters for Israel. From the time Joshua leads the people into the land the city is called **Jebusi**, Joshua 18:28, or **Jebus**, Judges 19:10-11.

As is stated on the map the cities of refuge are **Kadesh, Shechem and Hebron** on the west of the Jordan River; and **Golan, Ramoth and Bezer** on the east of the Jordan; Joshua 20:7-9.

The second map shows the land as it was divided among the tribes of Israel. The sons of Joseph, **Ephraim and Manasseh**, inherit land instead of Joseph and Levi.

The geography of the land of the Conquest is very fascinating to me. The Lebanon Mountains, a continuation of the Taurus Mountains in the north, extend down on both sides of the Jordan River. The Lebanons are on the west and the Anti-Lebanons are on the east. Between these two mountain ranges lies the deepest gorge in the world. It is called **el Ghor**. From Mount Hermon in the northern Anti-Lebanons, being over 9,000 feet above sea level, this gorge drops to some 1,292 feet below sea level at the Dead Sea, which is another 1,300 feet deep. The continuation of the gorge, from the southern end of the Dead Sea to the east arm of the Red Sea, or Gulf of Akaba, is called the Arabah.

The Lebanons extend down through Palestine, through the wilderness to the west arm of the Red Sea, or Gulf of Suez.

Mount Carmel is a short spur of the Lebanon range that extends out into the Mediterranean Sea across from the Sea of Galilee. The valley on the northeast of Mt. Carmel is called the **Valley of Jezreel**. An extension of the valley is called the Plain of Esdraelon. The fortress city of Megiddo overlooks Esdraelon.

To the south of Mt. Carmel, along the coastal plain is the **Plain of Sharon**.

The **Sea of Galilee** is called **Chinnereth** in the Old Testament, Numbers 34:11; Joshua 13:27; **Lake Gennesaret**, Luke 5:1 and **Galilee or Tiberias**, John 6:1. It is 12 ½ miles long and 7 ½ miles at the widest and is 680 feet below sea level.

The **Jordan River** originates about half way between Damascus and the Mediterranean Sea. It flows down and empties into the Dead Sea. Between the Sea of Galilee and the Dead Sea the Jordan is 65 miles long, as the birds fly, and 200 miles long, as the fish swim. So you can imagine how much it curves and twists.

The Dead Sea is so called because nothing can live in it. It has no outlet and is said to be 25 percent solid substance. It is 48 miles long and 10 miles at the widest.

Looking across the land from west to east we have the Coastal Plain, the Central Range, the Jordan Valley and the Eastern Range. Between the Coastal Range and the Central Range is a low range of mountains called the **Shephelah**. The Shephelah was a sort of buffer zone in the battles between Israel and the Philistines.

Goliath, no doubt, stood somewhere along the Shephelah as he chided the Israelites day and night, 1 Samuel 17. The Shephelah extended from the Plain of Sharon to Gaza.

Conquest

Joshua

To remember the name of the man who led the Israelites in the conquest, is to remember the name of the book in which that conquest is recorded; **Joshua**.

God's formula for success for Joshua is in Joshua 1:7-9. Joshua had for 40 years watched Moses adhere to the direct commands of God with great courage. **Moses had great influence on Joshua and Joshua was a good student.** Looking ahead for a moment, to the last days of Joshua's life, we hear him speaking these words to the people, **"Choose you this day whom ye will serve ... , but as for me and my house, we will serve the Lord,"** Joshua 24:15. Now we usually find this kind of enthusiasm at the beginning of one's life, but Joshua was as dedicated to God at the end of his life as at the beginning. We meet him leading in the first battle the Israelites confronted coming out of Egypt, Exodus 17; he is one of the two faithful spies sent into Canaan, Numbers 13, and he now has the distinction of leading the people into the Promised Land.

Notice how the people accept him from the very beginning, Joshua 1:16-18. A man cannot be a leader unless the people accept him as their leader. I am sure this was God's purpose of establishing Moses' leadership at the beginning of the wanderings, Numbers 12. He also had to convince the people that **Aaron** had been chosen to establish the priesthood, Numbers 16.

In Joshua 2 Joshua sends two spies into Canaan to the **city of Jericho**. Read the whole chapter and you will find these interesting facts. For 40 years the people of Jericho had been aware of how God, with great and mighty power, had guided and cared for this great multitude of people in the wilderness and brought them to within a very short distance away. **Over three million people are camped right across the Jordan River and the people of Jericho are terrified.** They knew about the crossing of the Red Sea, verse 10, also that the land of the Amorite and of Bashan had already been taken and their kings, **Sihon and Og,** had been killed. Of course this meant the entire eastern side of the Jordan had been taken and Jericho is right across the river on the west. Because of this the hearts of the people of Jericho have melted and there is no courage left in the city.

So when Joshua sent the two spies to Jericho, **Rahab** knew all about the Israelites and she did what she could to save her own family. She hid the men on her roof top. These cities were walled city kingdoms and the homes were built on top of the walls and they had flat roofs. **Someone had evidently seen the spies enter Rahab's house because the king knew where to look to find them.** Rahab readily admitted that the men had been in her home but that they had left before the gates of the city had been closed. She then pleaded with the spies to save her and her family when the city was taken. The spies make arrangements to save Rahab's family and then they return across the Jordan to Joshua. They tell Joshua that God has truly delivered this land into their hands. What a difference it would have made if the ten spies at Kadesh-barnea had joined Joshua and Caleb in giving the same type of report.

Three days later, Joshua crossed the Jordan River with the people. Even though it was the season for the Jordan to overflow its banks, Joshua 3:15-16, God caused the waters to part and the people cross over on dry ground as they did the Red Sea at 4 o'clock. **The river was backed up at the city of Adam, said to have been a mile below the Jabbok River, about eighteen miles north of Jericho.** The water was also held back where the Jordan flows into the Dead Sea. Jericho is not far from the Dead Sea so there must have been about twenty miles of dry land for the people to cross over.

Exactly half of the book of Joshua records the crossing of the Jordan to the conquest of the western side of the Jordan, Joshua 1-12. Joshua 12 gives the names of those kings captured and lands taken: verses 1-6, those on the east; verses 7-24, those on the west. The **conquest** of the eastern side of the Jordan is only referred to in Joshua. The conquest of these lands is recorded in Numbers and Deuteronomy. Only Joshua records the taking of the land on the west of the Jordan. Joshua 12:1 says the land taken on the east was from the river Arnon, east of the Dead Sea, to Mt. Hermon, northeast of the Sea of Galilee. **Mt. Hermon is one of the highest peaks of the Anti-Lebanon mountains**, being some 10,000 feet above sea level. It is said that the Dead Sea can be seen from Mt. Hermon, being about one hundred miles away.

It is far better to read, in one session, these first twelve chapters for the whole picture of the conquest of Canaan. Then after doing this, make notes on the conquest of the individual cities, with the activities surrounding them, for some of the most familiar stories of the Bible.

The conquest appears, on the surface, to be a very cruel undertaking. However, I believe the conquest has a very significant lesson for us today. God knew if these people, with their **cultures**, were left in the land, His own people would be led into **idolatry**; which was exactly what happened because the job wasn't thorough enough and lessons were not well learned by all. Does this sound familiar concerning our lives today? It is difficult, sometimes, to cut out of our lives all that offends, when we come to Jesus, leaving us unable to be wholly given to the cause for which He gave His all, the salvation of our own souls and the souls of those whom it is our responsibility to teach. A more miserable life cannot be imagined than to try to live with one foot in the church and one foot in the world. Both worlds are dim at best.

In Joshua 8:30-35 we have the scene of having the laws of blessings and cursings read from the book of the **Law of Moses**. Moses had given the instructions as to how they were to do this, in Deuteronomy 27. They were to set up great stones and plaster them, upon which they were to write these laws. The laws of blessings were to be read by the Levites from Mt. Gerizim and the laws of cursing from Mt. Ebal.

From Joshua 13-19 the land is divided by lot with **a special inheritance to Joshua and Caleb.** As you know, the Levites were to receive their inheritance from among the people. Also, Joseph's two sons, Ephraim and Manasseh, were to receive Joseph's inheritance so this would bring the number of the tribes back to twelve. On the east of the Jordan were two and one-half tribes; Reuben in the south, Gad in the central section and the half tribe of Manasseh in the north. So there were nine and one-half tribes on the west; Simeon, Judah, Benjamin and Dan in the south, with Caleb receiving the city of Hebron, Joshua 14:13.

In Genesis 13 when Lot "pitched his tent toward Sodom," Abraham and Sarah moved from Bethel to Hebron, Genesis 13:18. The central section of Canaan was allotted to Ephraim, the half tribe of Manasseh and Issachar, with a special inheritance of the city of Timnath-serah to Joshua, Joshua 19:49-50. In the north were the tribes of Zebulon, Asher, Naphtali and later, Dan.

The purpose of the six cities of refuge is given in Numbers 12; Deuteronomy 4:41-43. They are Kadesh in Naphtali, in the north; Shechem, the city that lay between Mt. Gerizim and Mt. Ebal, in Ephraim, in the central section; and Hebron, in Judah, in the southern section. These three cities were on the west side. On the east the cities were Bezer, in Reuben, in the south; Ramoth, in Gad, in the central section and Golan, in Manasseh, in the north. The cities are named in Joshua 20:7-9.

In Joshua 21 the Levites are given forty-eight cities among the tribes. Again, the three sons of Levi are always given to distinguish the families of the Levites. They are **Kohath, Gershon and Merari**. The Kohathites received thirteen cities from Judah, Simeon and Benjamin and ten cities from Dan, Ephraim and the half tribe of Manasseh, verses 4-5.

The Gershonites received thirteen cities from Issachar, Naphtali and the half tribe of Manasseh on the east, verse 6. The Merarites received twelve cities from Reuben and Gad on the east and Zebulon on the west, verse 7. Then the cities are named, verses 9-42.

The Lord then gives Israel **a period of peace** from the wars of the conquest, Joshua 21:43-45. Joshua dismisses the men of the tribes of Reuben, Gad and half tribe of Manasseh. They are allowed to cross over the Jordan to the east, where their families have waited out the conquest of Canaan, Joshua 22.

Joshua is an old man now and, as did Moses, he ends his life addressing the people to all that God has done for them. He exhorts them to love the Lord their God and serve Him only. The alternative is found in Joshua 23:13-16. As a matter of fact we see this very thing happening to the Israelites from toward the end of 9 o'clock through 11 o'clock.

Joshua refers to "the other side of the flood" in Joshua 24:2, yet this probably means the **Euphrates River**, as he goes on to mention Terah, Abraham and Nachor or Nahor. As he does not mention Haran, the other son of Terah, he is most likely thinking of the city of Haran. The American Standard Version renders this same phrase in verse 15, "beyond the river," and the phrase "the river" or "the great river," as in Joshua 1:4, always means the Euphrates; as "the great sea," Joshua 15:12, always means the Mediterranean.

Joshua had the people "witness against themselves," Joshua 24:21-26, and he set up a statute of this in **Shechem**. It is ironic that Shechem becomes the first capital city of the northern kingdom of Israel under Jeroboam and not one of these kings ever served God at any time.

Shiloh had become the spiritual headquarters of the Israelites. Gilgal was headquarters at the beginning, Joshua 4:1-19. So when the men of the Reubenites, Gadites and half tribe of Manasseh built a memorial altar at the Jordan, on their way home, all the people were disturbed, because only before the tabernacle was an offering to be made and only the Levites were to offer it. The explanation was then made that the altar had been built as a memorial and not for sacrifice.

Joshua had made his most memorable speech in Joshua 24:15, "Choose you this day whom ye will serve; .... as for me and my house, we will serve the Lord." **Joshua then dies at the age of 110**, verse 29. The bones of Joseph, which had been brought up from Egypt, Genesis 50:24-25, were buried in Shechem, which by the way, was in the territory given to Manasseh, son of Joseph.

To outline the book of Joshua for your deeper study of the details and to help remember where to pinpoint particular information, consider the following:

Joshua 1: Instructions to Joshua: the key to a successful conquest, verses 5-8.

Joshua 2-12: The conquest of the land. Make notes on the taking of each of the city kingdoms. Some are described vividly, such as:

The fall of Jericho, chapters 2 and 6; Ai and the sin of Achan, chapters 7-8; Confederated kings, the sun stood still for an extra day, chapters 9-10.

Joshua 13-22: The division of the land by lot. Special inheritance by Joshua and Caleb. The six cities of refuge and the forty-eight cities for the Levites.

Joshua 22-24: Shiloh becomes religious center; the tabernacle set up. Joshua's final address to the people. The death of Joshua.

- STUDY NOTES -

- STUDY NOTES -

IX. 7 o'clock
JUDGES

The Time of the Judges
Judges
Ruth

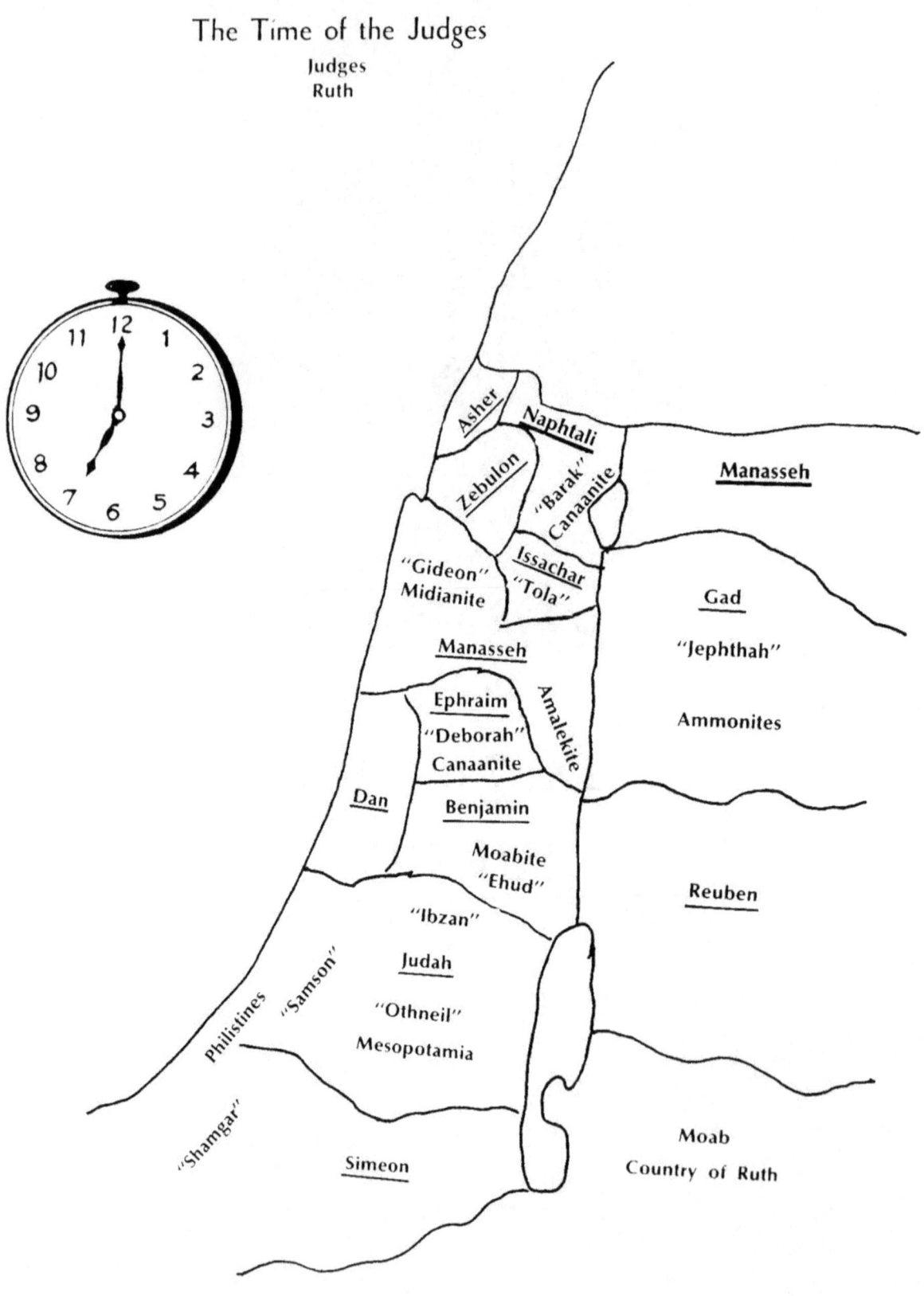

Judges

In the north, the people of the tribe of **Naphtali** were oppressed by the Canaanites, as was the tribe of Ephraim. **Deborah**, the only woman judge, and Barak led the battle against the Canaanites.

Gideon led in the fight against the Moabites and Amalekites; from the tribe of Manasseh. Ehud, from the tribe of Ephraim, also fought the Moabites.

Jephthah led in the battle against the Ammonites; from the tribe of Gad.

Othniel, the first Judge, from the tribe of Judah, fought against those of Mesopotamia, as did **Ibzan**.

Samson, the most familiar judge, to most people, fought against the Philistines, as did **Shamgar**.

You will want to make further notations on your map as you go through the book of Judges.

The city of **Bethlehem** and the country of **Moab** will be the scenes for the book of **Ruth.**

Judges

Judges

The period of the Judges is found in the book of Judges. There were some fifteen men whom God raised up, after the death of Joshua, to lead His people. The period of the Judges lasted about 300 years.

Samuel was the last of these judges, however, he is connected more closely to the kings of the United Kingdom, so we will not be bringing him into this period. He is not mentioned in the book of Judges.

The book opens with a continuation of an effort, on the part of some, to complete the conquest of the land. As we read in Joshua, all the people had not been conquered.

In the first chapter we have a "one of a kind" story. This man was reaping exactly what he had sown. **Judah and Simeon fought together against the Canaanites.** Adoni-bezek, king of Bezek, was captured and his thumbs and big toes were cut off. This punishment would seem at first to be peculiar with this king, and yet it must have been a common practice among the Canaanites. It appears, from verse 7, that Adoni-bezek had done the same thing to seventy of his own captives; and now he is the victim of the same cruelty.

Judges 1 also tells how each tribe failed to drive out the people in their allotted territory. The results are in Judges 2. **One generation after the death of Joshua, the people had forgotten God and had turned to the idols of the Canaanites, Judges 2:10-11.** How soon they had forgotten the pledge they had made in Shechem, Joshua 24.

Beginning in Judges 3, God, because of the cry of the people, verse 9, began to raise up Judges to lead the people in their battles against their oppressors. These men served only in their own territories, against particular people. No one Judge led all the people at one time. Some of them served simultaneously, only in different areas. **Othniel**, nephew of Caleb, was the first Judge, Judges 3:9-11. As will be noticed as we go along, the activities of some of the Judges are described in vivid color, while some are just mentioned by name and the fact they served as a Judge. You will want to read through and make your own notes.

The following is a list of the Judges, where they are found and the source of the immediate problem.

1. **Othniel,** Judges 3:9-11: **Mesopotamia**. Othniel was the nephew and son-in-law of Caleb.

2. **Ehud,** Judges 3:12-30: **Moab**. Read how this left-handed Judge handles Eglon, king of Moab. Remember that the Moabites are descendants of Lot, Genesis 19: 30-38, as were the Ammonites. The Amalekites, descendants of Esau, Genesis 36: 12, were also the oppressors at this time.

3. **Shamgar,** Judges 3:31: **Philistines**.

4. & 5. **Deborah and Barak**, Judges 4-5- **Canaanites**. This is one of the more vivid stories. Be sure to read why it was that a woman should be the instrument of victory over Jabin, the Canaanite king. Judges 5 is the victory song of Deborah and Barak.

6. **Gideon**, Judges 6-8:32: **Midianites**. Remember that the Midianites are the descendants of Abraham by Keturah, his wife after Sarah's death. They had six sons; one of them being Midian. Of the Judges, this is one you will be expected to know the details of, after having gone through the book. Do read this one and make notes. Notice the powerful forces of the enemy, Judges 6:5, and the number of men God told Gideon he would need to win the battle; and how they were chosen, Judges 7:1-7.

7. **Abimelech,** Judges 9: **Gideon**, or **Jerubbaal** as he was also called, Judges 7:1, had seventy-one sons, one by a concubine in Shechem whose name was Abimelech, Judges 8:30-31. This Judges 9

tells of Abimelech's treachery in trying to make himself Judge of the people. Read how he does this and the miserable estate of the Shechemites for having chosen him, in the parable of Jotham, only brother to escape his treachery, Judges 9:7-20.

8. & 9. Tola and Jair, Judges 10:1-5.

10. Jephthah, Judges 11-12: **Ammonites**. Jephthah was the illegitimate son of Gilead and is turned out of his house by his half-brothers. Later, the very people who turned him away ask him to lead them in their fight against the Ammonites. Read Jephthah's foolish promise to God in exchange for a victory over the Ammonites.

11, 12. & 13. Ibzan, Elon and Abdon, Judges 12:8-15.

14. Samson, Judges 13-16: **Philistines**. By far the longest and most vivid of all the Judges is the story of Samson. Here we have one of the most familiar stories of the Bible. If the world knows nothing else about the Bible, it knows this story. I am sure the movies of the story of Samson and Delilah have been shown all around this globe of ours. Of course you will want to make your own notes of this story.

After Samson, there was a time when "every man did that which was right in his own eyes," a sad state when you read such things as happened in Judges 19. Notice that it was the Benjamites who were behind the awful deed of Judges 19. Then notice that the other tribes almost annihilate the tribe of Benjamin. We will be referring back to this fact at 10 o'clock.

- STUDY NOTES -

- STUDY NOTES -

STUDY NOTES

X. 7:30 o'clock
RUTH

Ruth

Ruth

It was during the period of the Judges that the things of the book of Ruth take place. **The purpose of the book is to introduce the family who is to produce the greatest king of Israel, David.** It is a welcome narration at this time. The last two books have contained so much bloodshed. As needful as the fighting was, it is a welcome relief to now read the book of Ruth.

God called Abraham and with this one man started a chosen people from whom the Savior of the world would come. From this one man came a family; from the family came a nation; from this nation one tribe and now, in the book of **Ruth**, that tribe is narrowed down to one family again. **At 8 o'clock the family will culminate in one man, David. The Messiah is to come from the seed of David.**

Elimelech, with his wife Naomi and their two sons, Mahlon and Chilion, moved from their home in Bethlehem to the country of Moab, because there was a famine in the land of Israel. The two boys marry two Moabite girls, Ruth and Orpah. Ruth was Mahlon's wife and Orpah was Chilion's wife, Ruth 4:10.

Elimelech and the two boys die within ten years in Moab. Naomi then decides to return to her own country. She is greatly loved by both her daughters-in-law. One, Ruth, decides to return to Bethlehem with Naomi. It is at this time that she uses the very well-known expression, **"Entreat me not to leave thee, or to return from following after thee: for whither thou goest, I will go; and where thou lodgest, I will lodge: thy people shall be my people, and thy God my God: Where thou diest, will I die, and there will I be buried: the Lord do so to me, and more also, if ought but death part thee from me,"** Ruth 1:16-17."

Ruth goes to work in the fields of Boaz, a very wealthy kinsman of Elimelech. Read their love story and see how Boaz obtains Ruth for his wife, Ruth 2-4. Remember at 5 o'clock we outlined the book of Deuteronomy and in Deuteronomy 25:5-10 there were laws concerning taking on the responsibilities of caring for the wife of a brother who had died. At that time we looked ahead for a moment to the story of Ruth and Boaz. **From the marriage of Boaz and Ruth comes Obed, who was grandfather to King David.** The lineage of David, Ruth 4:17-22, is the purpose of the book.

This book also calls special attention to the city of Bethlehem for the first time. It will be the city in which David will be born, and long after David is gone, Micah, the prophet, says that it is out of Bethlehem that the Messiah will come, Micah 5:2-9.

- STUDY NOTES -

- STUDY NOTES -

XI. 8 o'clock
UNITED KINGDOM

The United Kingdom
1-2 Samuel
1 Kings 1-11

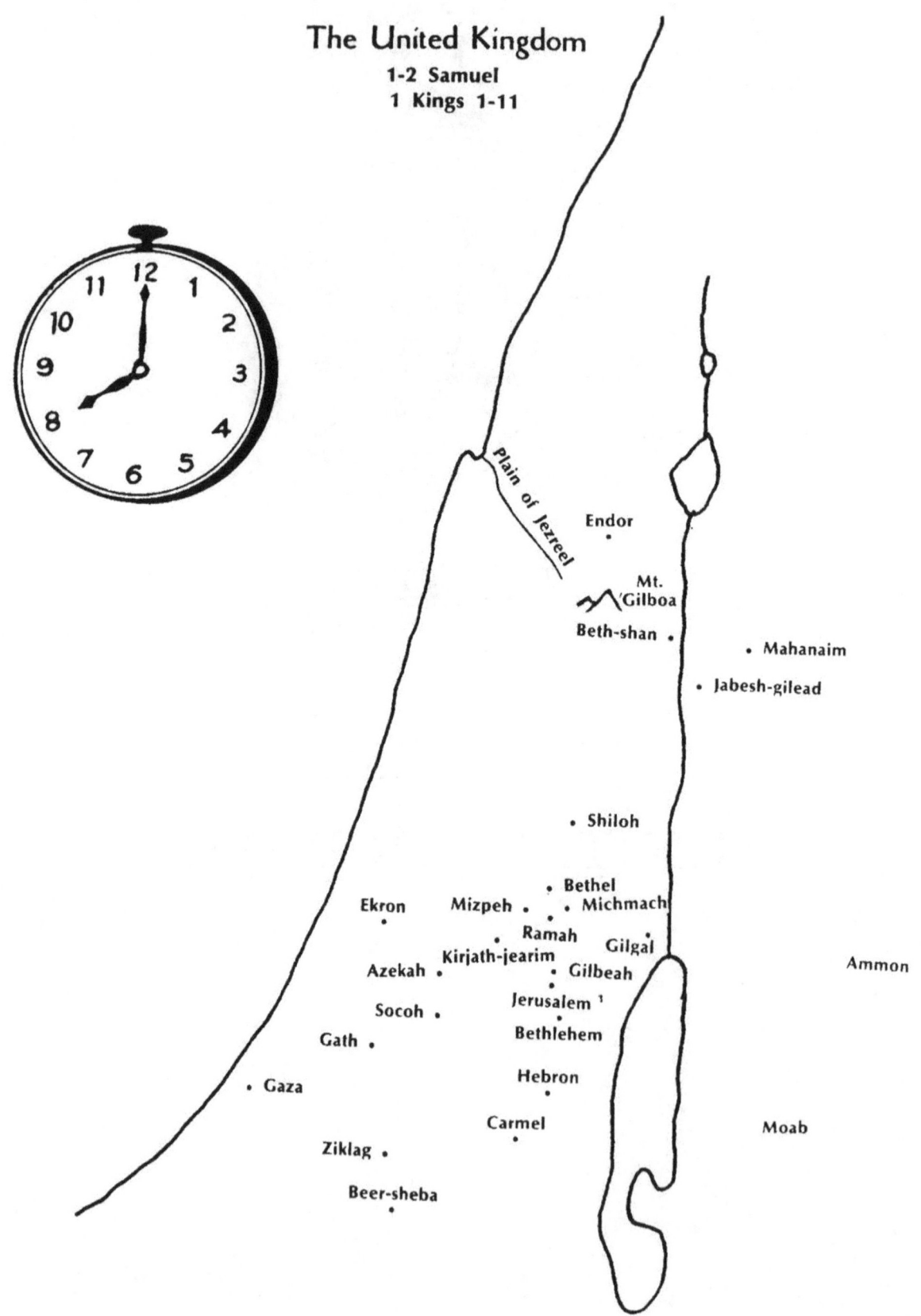

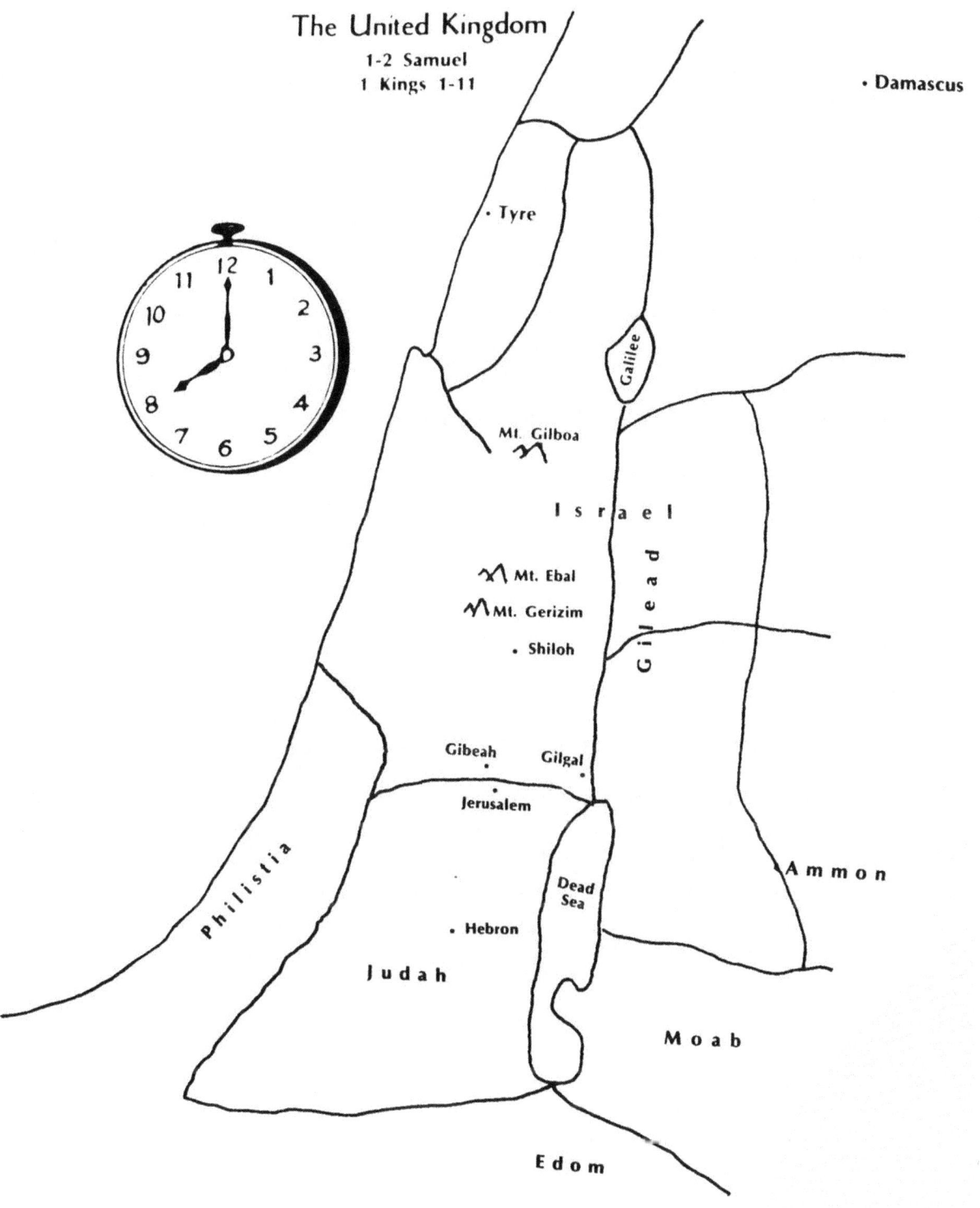

Geography

On the first map for this period there are just a few of the cities mentioned as you read the lives of Samuel, Saul and David. The most familiar ones will be:

Ramah, hometown of Samuel.

Gibeah, hometown of Saul, and evidently his capital.

Bethlehem, hometown of David.

Jerusalem, or **Jebus**, as it was called before David captured it and made it his capital.

Mt. Gilboa was the scene of the battle that took the lives of Saul and Jonathan.

Beth-shan: the bodies of Saul and Jonathan were put on display in Beth-shan.

Jabesh-gilead was the city for which Saul fought his first battle after becoming king. The inhabitants of Jabesh-gilead go to Beth-shan and get the bodies of Saul and Jonathan and bury them in their city.

Hebron was David's capital for 7 years while he was king over just Judah.

Endor was where Saul went to consult the witch.

Kirjath-jearim was where David went to get the Ark of the Covenant to bring it to Jerusalem.

Mahanaim was where David fled to when Absalom tried to usurp the throne.

On the second map you will note that Judah and Israel are divided. Saul reigned over all Israel, which included Judah. David reigned over just Judah for the first seven of his forty years as king. While king of all Israel, David expanded the land of Israel to include Edam, Moab, Ammon and Syria. Solomon, then, extended the boundaries north of Syria and east to the Euphrates River.

United Kingdom
1-2 Samuel
1 Kings 1-11

In the first chapter of 1 Samuel we read of the birth of the last Judge of Israel. It is a very poignant story. The man, Elkanah, of the tribe of Levi, 1 Chronicles 6:25, had two wives, **Hannah and Peninnah**. Peninnah had born Elkanah sons and daughters, but Hannah was unable, at this time, to bare children. Every year the family would go to Shiloh to make the annual sacrifice. The high priest over the tabernacle at this time was Eli and he had two sons named **Hophni and Phinehas.** In the eating of the things that Elkanah had brought, Deuteronomy 12:17-18, he gave Peninnah and her children portions but to Hannah he gave a double portion because he loved her: reminds me of Jacob with Rachel and Leah. However, because she could not bare Elkanah children, Peninnah taunted Hannah year after year. Hannah wept, not because she was taunted, but because she could not bare Elkanah a son.

One year at Shiloh Hannah prayed so fervently, but not aloud, that **Eli** thought she was drunk and told her to put away her wine, so she explained to him her great grief. Eli then uttered his own words of hope that God would grant her petition. Eli is to bless the day that that first boy is born.

Hannah, in her prayer to God, said that if she could bare a son she would give him up to the service of God for all of his life. The family returned to Ramah, and the Lord remembered Hannah; she conceived and bare a son and she called him Samuel, **"Because I asked him of the Lord,"** 1 Samuel 1:20. **Samuel means "heard of God."** That year when Elkanah went up to Shiloh Hannah did not go with him, for the reason given in 1 Samuel 1:22. In regards to the weaning time, in 2 Chronicles 31:16 it says of the Levites, 3 years and upward: ages five and twelve have also been suggested. At any rate we know that Samuel was a child when Hannah took him to Shiloh. She had promised to give him to the Lord all the days of his life, 1 Samuel 1:11, so that would mean from the earliest acceptable time. It also says, 1 Samuel 2:19, that Hannah made him a little cloak, denoting the size. She took the cloak when they went for the yearly sacrifice.

The year they took Samuel to stay, Eli blessed them and said, **"The Lord give thee seed of this woman for the loan that is lent to the Lord."** So Hannah was blessed with three more sons and two daughters, 1 Samuel 2:21.

In 1 Samuel 2:12-17, 22, we see the character of Eli's sons, Hophni and Phinehas. An otherwise unknown prophet comes to Eli and tells him that his family will be cut off from the priesthood because he had not taken care of his sons and their wicked ways. Both at his sons are to die in one day.

One night at Shiloh the Lord calls to Samuel while he sleeps, 1 Samuel 3. He thinks it is Eli calling him. After going to Eli the third time, Eli realized it was the Lord calling Samuel. Eli told Samuel to answer the next call with, **"Speak Lord, for thy servant heareth,"** verse 9. Samuel also is told that Eli's house is under judgment. The next morning Eli compels Samuel to tell him any and everything that the Lord had spoken to him. Samuel told him everything and Eli is reconciled to what will happen, verse 18.

Samuel grew in stature in such a way that all Israel, from Dan in the north to Beer-sheba in the south, knew that God had established him a prophet.

In 1 Samuel 4, in a battle with the Philistines, the Israelites were suffering great defeat. Hophni and Phinehas take it upon themselves to take the **Ark of the Covenant** to the battlefield. The Israelites were still defeated, Hophni and Phinehas are killed and the Philistines capture the ark. When Eli heard what had happened to his sons and the ark, he fell backward off his seat and the fall broke his neck and he died at the age of ninety eight, verse 15. The wife of Phinehas was expecting a baby and when she heard about her husband, about the ark and her father-in-law, she immediately went into labor, her child is born, and she died in childbirth. Before she dies she names her son Ichabod, which means **"inglorious"** for the reason that glory had been taken from Israel because the ark had been taken, verses 21-22.

Read 1 Samuel 5 to see what happens during the seven months the ark is in **Ashdod in Philistia**. The Philistines set the ark up in a temple alongside their God, Dagon; for which they are sorry: a story with a bit of humor in the beginning but ends with great misery for the Philistines. In 1 Samuel 6 we see that everyone suffers in every place the ark is taken until it reaches Kirjath-jearim; from where David later recovers it. Read this chapter and watch the procedure the Philistines go through to get the ark out of their country.

Sometime along the way, although we are not given the details, Samuel marries and has two sons, **Joel and Abijah,** who acted as judges in Beer-sheba. His sons, as Eli's sons, were not the men their fathers were, 1 Samuel 8:1-3. **It is at this time that the people ask for a king.** Samuel tries to warn them what they can expect from a king, verses 10-18; nevertheless they want a king, verse 19. As we are introduced to the young man who is to be Israel's first king, 1 Samuel 9:1-14, Samuel already knows how to recognize the man, verses 15-16. **Samuel anoints Saul as king, 1 Samuel 10:1, and he tells him how he himself will know and understand that he is God's choice, verses 2-12.** Samuel then makes it known to all the people, at Mizpah, that Saul, son of Kish, will rule over them as king, verses 17-24.

Those who are not pleased with Saul as king, 1 Samuel 10:27, change their minds after seeing how Saul handles the Ammonites, 1 Samuel 11. Nahash, the Ammonite, threatened the people of **Jabesh-gilead**, a city in Gad, east of the **Jordan River**. In trying to co-exist with the Ammonites, the people of Jabesh-gilead were under the threat of having their right eyes plucked out as a sign that Israel had been disgraced. Asking for seven days to make the decision whether or not to accept such a condition, the elders of Jabesh-gilead send messages throughout Israel asking for help. As Saul was coming home from the fields he heard the **people of Gibeah** weeping. In asking what the trouble was, he was told about Jabesh-gilead. In Saul's anger he took a pair of oxen, cut them into pieces and sent them throughout Israel with the message that the same thing would happen to the oxen of any who refused to come to the aid of the people of Jabesh-gilead. The response was abundantly favorable and Jabesh-gilead was saved. At the death of Saul we find the people of Jabesh-gilead retrieving the bodies of Saul and his three sons and burying them in their city, 1 Samuel 31:11-13.

After the battle over Jabesh-gilead, all the people gather at **Gilgal** and renew the selection of Saul as king, 1 Samuel 11:14-15.

From 1 Samuel 11-15, we see the rise and fall of the first king of Israel. There are diversities of sin, and the sins of Saul, which caused his downfall, were sins of presumption. **Notice in 1 Samuel 13:7-14 how he presumed a sacrifice offered by him, king of all Israel, would be acceptable. Of course, it was not. Only the Levites were to function as priests in the offering of sacrifices.** Saul was told the kingdom would be taken from him, verse 14. Again, notice in 1 Samuel 15 how he presumed it was all right to save the cattle of the Amalekites if they were for the purpose of sacrifice, even though God's command was total destruction of the Amalekites, verse 3. Samuel's words to Saul were these, **"Behold, to obey is better than sacrifice,"** verse 22.

Again he is told that the kingdom will be taken from him, verse 28. We need to be very careful in our own lives that we do not presume that it is alright to do something just because it seems a good thing, as Saul did in offering the sacrifice; in itself a very righteous thing, except it was contrary to the will of God for Saul to do it. **We want also to be careful about doing things because it seems reasonable to us, as Saul saving the cattle for sacrifice, even though God had said to destroy everything.** Anything we do in adherence to the will of God does not go unnoticed, nor does anything we do contrary to the will of God go unnoticed. Can we lose the kingdom today with a sin of presumption? I think we can. Only a knowledge of God's will and an adherence to it will suffice.

In 1 Samuel 16:1-13 a new king is anointed. Even though Samuel knows that Saul has sinned, he grieves for him. God lifts him out of that grief by giving him the job of anointing a new king; **"a man after God's own heart,"** 1 Samuel 13:14 and Acts 13:22. Samuel knows the heart of Saul and knows that Saul would kill him if he knew he was preparing to anoint a new king, read 1 Samuel 16:14. So God shows Samuel how to successfully handle the situation, 1 Samuel 16:2-3. In Eliab, the oldest son of Jesse, Samuel evidently sees another Saul, the Saul as he was when he was chosen to be king, 1 Samuel 9:2. However, it says, 1 Samuel 16:7, **"man looks on the outward appearance, but the Lord looks on the heart."** Three of the seven older sons of Jesse brought before Samuel are named; **Eliab, Abinadab and Shammah**. After seeing these and the Lord had not given him any sign that the new king was among them, Samuel asked Jesse if these seven were all of his sons. Jesse tells Samuel he has one younger son, and David is sent for. When David appeared, God told Samuel to arise and anoint him. So David was anointed king of Israel. He does not reign as king, however, until the death of Saul. Saul continues to live throughout the last half of this book of 1 Samuel, but for the most part it is David's life in 1 Samuel 16-31. Saul comes into the picture as he touches the life of David.

To study the life of David in such a way as to remember just where to turn to locate a certain **sequence**, consider the following:

1 Samuel 16-17: David as a lad.

1 Samuel 18-20: David in the court of Saul.

1 Samuel 21-31: David, the outlaw.

2 Samuel 1- 4: David, king of Judah only.

2 Samuel 5-24: David, king of all Israel.

In the same chapter that David is anointed king we also discover that he is a musician. In 1 Samuel 16:14 it says that the Spirit of God had left Saul and that God had sent an evil spirit to trouble him. A servant suggested that Saul seek out a man to sooth his spirit with the harp. Another servant knew about David, and David was sent for. Saul does not know that the man who is to take his place as king of Israel is his harpist.

1 Samuel 17 tells of David's fight with Goliath, the Philistine giant. If you will notice, the Philistines are the oppressors, for the most part, of the Israelites in 1 Samuel. Of Jesse's eight sons, only the three who are named are old enough to go to war, read Numbers 1:3. **So there are four brothers between these and David, so David couldn't have been over 15 or 16 years of age when he killed Goliath.** Goliath had come out on the mountain every morning and every evening for forty days to taunt the Israelites with the idea that they did not have one man of the stature to fight him. Jesse had sent David out to the battlefield with food for his older brothers.

When he sees Goliath and understands what is going on, these are his words, **"Who is this uncircumcised Philistine, that he should defy the armies of the living God?"** David tells Saul that he will fight Goliath. When he met Goliath he said, **"You come out against me with a spear and a shield, but I come against you in the name of the Lord of hosts, the God of the armies of Israel, whom you have defiled,"** verse 45. Then in verse 47 he says, **"All this assembly shall know that the Lord saveth not with sword and spear: for the battle is the Lord's, and He will give you into my hands."** The sling and a pebble were as near to nothing that David could use to show that the battle was, in fact, God's.

1 Samuel 18 discloses the love that existed between David and **Jonathan**, son of Saul. David went to live in Saul's house. He is very popular with everyone, those who served under him in battle as well as all of Saul's servants.

Coming home from a battle with the Philistines, David is greeted by the women with a song that starts Saul on an insane rampage to kill David, a rampage that lasts for the rest of Saul's life. The words of the song the women were singing were these, **"Saul hath slain his thousands and David his ten thousands,"** verse 7. Saul tries several times to "pin David against the wall" with his spear. He relieved him of the playing of the harp and instead put him in charge of a thousand soldiers, hoping he would be killed in battle. It was certainly not because of Saul's love for David that he wanted him for a son-in-law. It was through the cost of obtaining **Michal**, the king's daughter, for his wife, that Saul again hoped David would be killed. Read the price Saul set on his daughter, 1 Samuel 18:25-27.

In 1 Samuel 19 Jonathan tries to persuade his father to put out of his mind the idea of killing David, verses 1-6. However, with the next successful battle David has against the Philistines, Saul again tries to "pin David against the wall" with his spear, verses 9-10. **Then Michal saves David's life, verses 11-18.** David then goes to the city of Ramah to Samuel. Samuel and David go to Naioth, the school of prophets in Ramah. Read how Saul tries to kill David at Naioth, verses 18-24.

Jonathan couldn't believe that his father was still bent on destroying David, 1 Samuel 20. He and David devise a plan to find out once and for all what Saul's intentions are concerning David. When Saul tries to kill his own son, Jonathan, for taking David's part in the situation, Jonathan is convinced that his father will not be content with anything short of the death of David.

Jonathan then lets David know that he must leave Saul's house forever. David and Jonathan weep together and renew their covenant to care for one another's families, 1 Samuel 20:8-17, 41-42. These two young men only met one other time after this parting. In 1 Samuel 23:16-18, Jonathan tells David that he is certain that his father will not succeed in his effort to kill David and that he will live to reign as king over all Israel. Furthermore, he says, his father also knows this.

From 1 Samuel 21-31 David is a fugitive. He has an army of misfits, numbering about six hundred, 1 Samuel 23:13. In 1 Samuel 21:1-6 we have the incident that Jesus refers to in Matthew 12:3-4 and Mark 2:23-26. David goes to **Nab**, a city of priests, and asks Ahimelech, the priest, for the hallowed bread for him and his men to eat. On that same day a servant of Saul's, named **Doeg**, was there. It was because of Doeg, and by him, that Ahimelech, along with all the priests and their families, was killed, 1 Samuel 22:9-19. Only one of Ahimelech's sons, Abiathar, escapes, verses 20-23.

As Saul is in pursuit of David, David has two opportunities to kill Saul, but he can't bring himself to kill God's anointed, 1 Samuel 24; 26. Both times Saul makes a beautiful speech to David, 1 Samuel 24:16-22; 1 Samuel 26:21-25. After making the first speech Saul continues his pursuit of David, but after the second speech he pursues him no more, 1 Samuel 27:4.

The familiar story of Saul going to the witch at **Endor** is in 1 Samuel 28. Although he himself had put away all those who had a "familiar spirit," Saul finds his only source of help is in a witch. He has gathered his army at Gilboa to fight his last battle. He prays to God, but God does not answer him. He then turns to the witch. **Endor is a city just north of Mt. Gilboa, not far from the Sea of Galilee.** He asks the witch to bring forth the spirit of Samuel, who has died, 1 Samuel 25:1. Samuel comes forth all right, but it is a great shock to this woman, the fake that she is, and she is afraid for her life. Saul tells Samuel that he is in trouble and that he has prayed to God but that God will not answer.

Read Samuel's reply to Saul, 1 Samuel 28:16-19. The next day on Mt. Gilboa, Saul and his three sons, Jonathan, Abinadab and Melchishua, are slain. The people of Jabesh-gilead went to Beth-shan and took the bodies of Saul and his sons and buried them in Jabesh-gilead, 1 Samuel 31:11-13.

For a bird's-eye view of 1 Samuel, consider the following:

a. The birth and life of Samuel, the last Judge.

b. The life of Saul as first king of Israel.

c. The first three phases of David's life; as a lad, in the court of Saul, and as a fugitive.

Looking ahead for a moment, and in order to have all the scripture has to offer for this portion of this 8 o'clock period, let's look at 12 o'clock. **As you will notice on the second clock, of the books of the Old Testament, the books at 12 o'clock are Ezra, Esther and Nehemiah with 1-2 Chronicles.** Ezra compiled the books of 1-2 Chronicles after the captivity for the purpose of re-establishing things in their original state; land to the rightful owners and the order of worship in the temple according to the families of the Levites.

The books of 1-2 Chronicles cover the same periods of history as does 1-2 Samuel and 1-2 Kings, although from 9 o'clock to 12 o'clock they pertain primarily to the southern kingdom of Judah; the family of David. So for any added information of 1 Samuel turn to 1 Chronicles 1-10. For the most part these chapters are genealogies, beginning with Adam and ending with the Restoration. **However, they are important to read to see, once again, one of the frameworks within which we are building our knowledge of the Old Testament.** You will always remember where you read these lineages, even though they are not the most interesting portion of the Old Testament. Our goal is to be able to put our finger on any information we might need.

Psalms

The title for this book is from the Septuagint, the Greek Old Testament. Its title in Hebrew means "Praises."

The history of the psalms extends from the Exodus at 4 o'clock, to the Restoration at 12 o'clock. Then there are those psalms which are Messianic, fulfilled in Christ. Jesus said, "All things must be fulfilled which were written in the Law of Moses, and in the prophets, and in the psalms, concerning me," Luke 24:44.

Psalms 90 is the earliest in point of time, written by Moses.

The reason for bringing your attention to this book at this time is that about half of these psalms were written by David, and they are more readily understood if considered in the light of their historical background. It would be most profitable to have a good outline of the book of Psalms in front of you as you study the life of David.

You will know and understand how this man, who sinned greatly in the eyes of God, could still be called **"a man after God's own heart."** David pours his very soul into these psalms, mostly in thanksgiving, praise, trust and faith, as well as in penitence and guidance. You will find David's name prefixed to those psalms written by him. Check through and make your own outline if one is not available to you. You will be glad you attuned your mind to the book of Psalms in this fashion and at this time.

David, King of Judah
2 Samuel 1-4

As David returns from a battle with the **Amalekites** to Ziklag, a young man came to him with the news of the battle on Mt. Gilboa. He tells David that Saul and Jonathan are dead and that the rest of the army is either dead or they have fled from the battle area. If this young man thought he could get on the good side of David by fabricating this story of how Saul died, 2 Samuel 1:4-10, he was in for a rude awakening, verses 13-16.

David then gives the words to a song to be taught all the children of Judah, 2 Samuel

1:19-27. **David paid great honor to a man who had sought repeatedly to take his life.** He felt about Saul the same way Samuel felt about him, 1 Samuel 15: 35. Saul had been the Lord's anointed and David respected that fact. David's heart also made the difference. At the end of David's life we won't look back on a sinless man; David sinned greatly, but we do look back on the life of a man who was keenly aware of his sins and always went to his God in all humility, begging from the bottom of his heart for understanding and forgiveness. We need only to read the Psalms of David to know the heart of David.

Now that Saul is dead, David prays to God for guidance as to his future as king. He knows he is to reign as king of Israel and yet he shows great patience in this coming about. God told David to go over into Judah to the city of **Hebron**. There the people of the tribe of Judah make him king over Judah, 2 Samuel 2:1-7. He is king of Judah for 7 ½ years, 2 Samuel 5:4-5. During these years two incidents stand out in my mind. Read about **Abner** who had been commander of Saul's army and Joab, commander of David's army, 2 Samuel 2:8-3:39.

Then read the fate of **Ishbosheth**, son of Saul, 2 Samuel 4:1-12. Notice that David deals with the murderers of Ishbosheth the same way he dealt with the young Amalekite who thought he was serving David by claiming to have killed Saul, 2 Samuel 1:1-15 and 2 Samuel 4:9-12. Notice also the mention of Mephibosheth, crippled son of Jonathan, 2 Samuel 4:4. There will be more about him later.

Before David went to Hebron he had three wives. **Michal**, daughter of Saul, 1 Samuel 18:27; 19:11-17, had been given to another man after David fled from the house of Saul, 1 Samuel 25:44. He also married **Abigail**, Nabal's wife, 1 Samuel 25; and **Ahinoam**, 1 Samuel 25:43. He went to Hebron with just Abigail and Ahinoam, 2 Samuel 2:2. During the 7 ½ years he was king of Judah, he married four more women, 2 Samuel 3:1-5. Six of these seven wives bore David six sons. Of these six sons we become most familiar with **Amnon and Absalom**, 2 Samuel 13-19; and **Adonijah**, 1 Kings 1-2:25.

Ishbosheth and Abner had their differences, 2 Samuel 3:7-10, and **Abner** notified David that he was ready to be of service to him that he might be established king of all Israel. David told Abner he could start helping him by bringing **Michal** to him, verse 13. When Abner brought Michal to him, David prepared a great feast for Abner and his men and assured him there was peace between them. It is right after this feast that **Joab**, commander of David's army, kills Abner, verses 22-29. There is great mourning over the death of Abner. David must have had great respect for the man who had served Saul so well.

After Abner's death, Ishbosheth lost all courage to continue the battle between the house of Saul and the house of David. He is then slain by his own men, in his bed, 2 Samuel 4:5-12.

David, King of All Israel
2 Samuel 5-24

The elders of all the tribes went to David in Hebron and made him king over all Israel. He had reigned over Judah for 7 ½ years. He is at this time still a very young man, only 30 years old. He has been king since he was twenty-three. **He is to live to reign over Israel 33 years, making a total of 40 years as king, 2 Samuel 5:5.** Each of the three kings of the United Kingdom reigned for 40 years.

The first thing David does as king of Israel is capture the city of Jerusalem. He makes that city his official residence. He erects a tent and goes and reclaims the Ark of the Covenant, 2 Samuel 6, where we read of **Uzzah**, who reached out his hands to keep the ark from falling and died on the spot. God had said only certain ones were to handle the things of the tabernacle, verses 1-6.

David felt guilty about living in such a fine home, 2 Samuel 7:2, and the ark dwelling in a tent. He spoke to **Nathan** the prophet and Nathan told him to go ahead and do whatever he wanted to about it because God was with him. However, that night God told Nathan that His house is not of this world, that He will build His house in His own way, 2 Samuel 7:12-13. Nathan tells David and David accepts God's decision.

In 2 Samuel 8, God goes with David in his efforts to subdue all the countries close around him.

David wants to know if there is any of the house of Saul left and he is told that there is a son of Jonathan who is lame in his feet, read 2 Samuel 4:4. David sent for **Mephibosheth**, who at first wonders just what his fate is, 2 Samuel 9:6. David assures him that because he is Jonathan's son he is to be shown great kindness. David restores all that belonged to Saul to Mephibosheth, who lives in the house of David as a son, verse 11. He left **Ziba** and his sons to care for the property that belonged to Mephibosheth.

This **Nahash** of 2 Samuel 10:2 is the king who came against Jabesh-gilead when Saul took such a strong stand, 1 Samuel 11. We are not sure just when this man showed kindness to David unless it was when David was a fugitive and fled to Moab, 1 Samuel 22:1-4. The **Moabites and Ammonites,** remember, were brothers, sons of Lot. Their land joined on the east of the Dead Sea. Anyway, we see that David's good intentions were met with suspicion, and a battle results.

I suppose of all the stories of the Bible there is not one more widely known than the story of David and Bathsheba, 2 Samuel 11-12. In the New Testament, in Hebrew 8:12; 10:17, we read, "And their sins and iniquities will I remember no more." However, I believe there is a constructive remembrance. **I believe that God forgave David of every transgression that he confessed; and it seems from the Psalms of David that he reached into the very depth of his mind and soul for those things that he had committed in every phase of his life, from his youth to his old age, to empty his life of all wrong doing and lay them at the mercy of his God.** However, to the mind of the prophet who wrote the accounts of 1-2 Samuel God reveals the sins of David for the whole world to know. So you see, God did not remember them against David. On the day of Pentecost, Peter spoke to some who had crucified Jesus; "whom ye have crucified," he said, in Acts 2:36. Now we know that all those who obeyed the command to repent and be baptized were forgiven of this terrible thing, but to the mind of Luke, the writer of the book of Acts, was given the details of their sin for all the world to know. So in this way I believe there is a constructive remembrance on the part of God.

We notice in 2 Samuel 11 that David had sinned in the first place for having taken **Bathsheba**, but we also see how this first sin started a snowball of sins on the part of David. When Bathsheba told David she was expecting his child, David called in **Uriah**, her husband, from the war and tried to get him to go home so he would think the child was his own. When that didn't work David wrote Uriah's death warrant and even had Uriah deliver his own death warrant to Joab, commander of David's army. David tried to cover his **sin of adultery** with the equally great **sin of murder**. That is just the way sin works in our lives when we try to cover it up. Also, the cost of sin is so great. We see that it cost David his little son born to him by Bathsheba, 2 Samuel 12:14-23. So you see, when we sin it hurts everyone involved with us.

One very important aspect of David's actions, however, after the death of his little son, that we should take notice of, is his faith in God's promises, 2 Samuel 7:17-29, even though he knew he had sinned greatly. When his servants couldn't understand how he could cope so well with the **death** of the child, while he had not been so able with the **illness** of the child, 2 Samuel 12:16-21, David said, **"While the child was yet alive, I fasted and wept: for I said, Who knoweth whether Jehovah will not be gracious to me, that the child may live? But now he is** dead, wherefore should I fast? Can I bring him back again? I shall go to him, but he will not return to me." David knew what God expects from one who sins. You need to turn, right now, to Psalm 6, 32, 51, to understand how he felt about his sins, and yet I read no hesitation in his statement, "I shall go to him." These are some of the great and wonderful lessons learned from the study of God's word in the Old Testament. It only enhances the prospect of our accepting the promises of the New Testament.

After the death of Uriah, David had made Bathsheba his wife, 2 Samuel 11:27. Bathsheba had other sons following the death of that first child; read 1 Chronicles 3:5. Also read Matthew 1:7 and Luke 3:31 and notice where Joseph's and Mary's lineages divide; Joseph from Solomon, son of David and Bath-sheba, and Mary from Nathan, son of David and Bathsheba.

In 2 Samuel 13 we find David reaping, among his children, what he had sown in his own life. Amnon was David's oldest son; Absalom was David's third son, son of Maachah, the daughter of the king of Geshur, a country just east of the Sea of Galilee. **Tamar** was Absalom's sister, both being the children of David and Maachah; Tamar was Amnon's half-sister. **Jonadab**, friend of Amnon, was also his cousin, being David's nephew. Read the chapter to learn how Amnon dishonored his half-sister Tamar, upon the advice of his cousin, Jonadab, and how Absalom, even after waiting 2 years avenges the wrong done to his sister. Notice also where he goes when he runs from his father's house, 2 Samuel 13:37-38; also 2 Samuel 3:3.

After 3 years, Joab figures out a way for Absalom to be allowed to at least **return to Jerusalem**, if not to his father's house, 2 Samuel 14:1-24. Joab was not only commander of David's army, he was also his nephew, son of his sister, **Zeruiah**, verse 1. These boys, David's sons and nephews, were close friends and yet to a point, as we will see later on with Joab and Absalom.

Absalom had all the outward appearances of the son of a king, 2 Samuel 14:25-26. He married and had three sons and one daughter whom he named after his sister, **Tamar**. After 2 years of living in Jerusalem and yet not allowed in his father's house, he uses Joab to help him take the first step in trying to usurp his father's throne, 2 Samuel 14:28-33.

In 2 Samuel 15 Absalom begins a well-planned, dedicated, concerted effort to become king of Israel, even if it cost the life of his father, David. First he stole the hearts of the people, verses 1-6, then he made his move to become king, verses 7-12. A messenger tells David what has transpired and David knows that Absalom will stop at nothing to gain the throne, verse 14, so he leaves Jerusalem, leaving ten concubines to run his house. He also persuades **Zadok** and **Abiathar**, the high priests, and **Hushai**, one of his counselors, to remain in Jerusalem to act on his behalf, verses 24-37. Then Absalom moves into the city.

Read 2 Samuel 16:20-22 to see the real character of Absalom. Then in 2 Samuel 17:2, he is ready also to take his father's life. **Ahithophel**, counselor to Absalom, suggests a plan to accomplish David's defeat. Absalom asks for the **counsel of Hushai** and accepts it. In trying to get the word to David by Ahimaaz and Jonathan, sons of Zadok and Abiathar, the two boys barely escape with their lives, verses 15-21.

Knowing that Absalom had not heeded his counsel, **Ahithophel** goes to his own city, to his home, sets his house in order and hangs himself, 2 Samuel 17:23.

David crossed over the Jordan River into Gilead to the town of Mahanaim. This was the city where **Ishbosheth**, son of Saul, declared himself king at the death of Saul.

Absalom has made his cousin, **Amasa**, commander of the army in the absence of Joab. They also passed over into Gilead. Both David and Absalom prepare for the battle ahead. **David had set Joab and his brothers Abishai and Ittai as commanders over his army.** David himself is persuaded not to lead the battle. He then commands that these three men deal gently with Absalom. During the battle Absalom's long hair gets caught in the bough of a tree and he is left hanging there. One of the men told Joab and Joab tries to get the man to kill Absalom. The man refuses, saying he heard the command given by the king. So Joab kills Absalom as he hangs there from the tree, throws him into a pit and covered the pit with stones, 2 Samuel 18:1-18. Absalom's three sons evidently preceded him in death, verse 18.

Ahimaaz, son of Zadok, wanted to be the one to break the news to David about Absalom, verse 19; however when the time came he wasn't anxious to give him the details, verses 28-29. Another messenger, who evidently wasn't so emotionally involved, was happy to tell David that the one who had sought his life was dead. Then we hear that very familiar lament of David over his favorite son, "0 my son Absalom, my son, my son Absalom; would I had died for thee, O Absalom, my son, my son."

When Joab hears how David is weeping and mourning over Absalom, he becomes very angry. He tells David that he has shamed the very people who had fought so hard to save the king and the nation of Israel; that David loved the one who had hated him and hated the ones who had loved him; that he would have been happy if everyone else had been killed, even his wives and other children, just so Absalom could have been kept alive, 2 Samuel 19:1-6. He tells David that the people are so discouraged they are ready to leave him, verse 7.

David is brought back to Jerusalem to a very shaky nation of people, making it possible for Sheba to attempt to usurp the throne. David has, in the meantime, made **Amasa** commander in Joab's place. When David called on Amasa to pursue Sheba, Joab, on the pretense of embracing him, kills Amasa with his sword, 2 Samuel 20:1-10. Sheba is beheaded in Abel-Beth- Maacah, a city of Naphtali, northwest of the Sea of Galilee.

2 Samuel 21 tells of three years of famine in the land. David prayed to God and God told him it was because of Saul's treatment of the **Gibeonites**. Remember when Joshua led the people into the Promised Land, the fear of all the people of Canaan as they saw this great multitude of people coming in, with great miraculous power? **The Gibeonites disguised themselves as people from a far-away land.** Joshua made a covenant with these people, read Joshua 9 to recall the incident. Notice verses 23 and 27 of Joshua 9. The Gibeonites were slaves in the service of the tabernacle. Now then, turn to 1 Samuel 22 and recall how Saul had had all the priests of the city of Nob slain, along with all the men, women, children and animals. This is the incident referred to by God.

David asks the Gibeonites what kind of retribution they required and it was life for life. Seven sons of Saul were slain that day. David recovers the bones of Saul and Jonathan from Jabesh-gilead and buries them with the seven in the sepulcher of Kish, father of Saul. The famine was then lifted from the land.

After another successful battle with the Philistines, David praised and thanked God in the words of a song, 2 Samuel 22:1-51. The words of these verses are typically David.

In the last chapter of 2 Samuel David orders Joab to **number the people**. In the first verse it says that the Lord, in His anger against Israel, moved David to do this. In 1 Chronicles 21:1, it says the idea was Satan's. In any case, the practice was to just number the army of Israel, see Numbers 1:3; 26:2. This was also David's purpose, verse 9. Of course David knew he had done the wrong thing, verse 10.

Through the prophet, **Gad**, God had him choose his own punishment. Of the three he was compelled to confront; his enemies, his people or God, he chose God. Again, for David's sin many others suffered: seventy thousand died in three days. When the angel raised his hand to smite the city of Jerusalem, God stopped him. The angel stood beside the **threshing floor of Araunah**.

David admitted the sin was his and retribution should be on his own house. Gad told David he was to build an altar on the threshing floor of Araunah. David offers to pay Araunah for his threshing floor. When Araunah offered to furnish everything for David's sacrifice, David said, **"Nay; but I will surely buy it of thee at a price: neither will I offer burnt offerings unto the Lord my God of that which doth cost me nothing."** David offers the sacrifice and the plague was stopped.

1 Chronicles 11-29

At the end of the survey of 1 Samuel there is a notation to look to 1 Chronicles 1-10 for additional information.

Now at the end of the survey of 2 Samuel we look to the rest of 1 Chronicles, chapters 11-29, for additional information concerning the reign of David as king of Judah and then of all Israel.

You will want to remember that 1-2 Chronicles were compiled by Ezra at 12 o'clock and deal primarily with the house of David. Just keep the following in mind:

For 1 Samuel also study 1 Chronicles 1-10.

For 2 Samuel also study 1 Chronicles 11-29 and also the Psalms of David;

For 1 Kings 1-11 also study 2 Chronicles 1-9 and also Proverbs, Ecclesiastes and Song of Solomon.

For 1 Kings 12-22 through 2 Kings 1-25 look to 2 Chronicles 10-36 for additional information of the kings of Judah only.

Solomon, King of Israel
1 Kings 1-11

As the book of 1 Kings opens, David is very old. **A young Shunamite girl named Abishag was brought in to minister to David.**

Adonijah, David's fourth son, assumes he is to be the next king, 1 Kings 2:15. The three older boys Amnon, Chileab and Absalom, are dead. Adonijah was, as his brother Absalom, a good looking man. He prepared himself a chariot and had fifty men run before him, as did his brother, Absalom. He tries to usurp the throne, with the help of Joab and Abiathar, the priest. He invites all the king's sons, except Solomon, also some of the servants, and declares himself king of Israel.

Nathan, the prophet, notifies Bathsheba what Adonijah is doing and the two of them tell David. David then arranges to have Solomon anointed king. **Even though Solomon was not in line to be king, he was God's choice, 1 Chronicles 22:9-10.** The noise of the celebration of Solomon becoming king is heard by Adonijah, Joab and all who were celebrating with Adonijah. Jonathan, son of Abiathar, told Adonijah that David had had Solomon anointed king, that Solomon rode on the king's mule and now sits on the throne, 1 Kings 1:42-46. All those with Adonijah are struck with fear and they all leave him. Adonijah himself is afraid of what Solomon might do to him. Solomon allows Adonijah to go home.

In 1 Kings 2 David dies. Before he dies he gives last minute charges to Solomon. His first concern is that he be faithful to God and His commandments which are in the Law of Moses; to remember the promise of God to him when He said, **"If thy children take heed to their way, to walk before me in truth with all their heart and with all their soul, there shall not fail thee, (said he), a man on the throne of Israel,"** verse 4.

Then David tells Solomon to bring judgment upon Joab for having slain Abner and Amasa; to show kindness to the sons of his good friend, **Barzillai**, of Gilead, who was so kind to him when he fled from Absalom, read 2 Samuel 19:31-39.

David had reigned as king for 40 years; 7 years in Hebron over Judah and 33 years in Jerusalem over all Israel, 1 Kings 2:10-11.

Adonijah appeals to Bathsheba for permission to have Abishag for his wife. When Bathsheba asks Solomon to give Abishag to Adonijah, Solomon is enraged. He has **Benaiah** kill Adonijah.

Abiathar, high priest with Zadok, had made the mistake of not abiding by the wishes of David as to his successor and went along with **Adonijah** in his attempt to become king. However, because he had served David well, Solomon just removes him from the priestly office. This is said to have ended the family of Eli in the priesthood, verse 27. Remember that **Abiathar** was the only one to escape the massacre brought on the priestly town of Nob by King Saul, 1 Samuel 22:20. In spite of the fact that Solomon seems to be relieving Abiathar of his priestly duties, he is still mentioned in 1 Kings 4:4 as priest.

In 1 Kings 2:28-35 we read of the **death of Joab** and Benaiah being made commander of the army in his place.

Remember **Shimei**, the man who had cursed and thrown stones at King David as he was fleeing from Absalom? He was of the family of Saul, 2 Samuel 16:5-14, and had, evidently, a long standing grudge against David. **When Absalom was killed and David was returning to Jerusalem, Shimei begged David's forgiveness.** David allowed him to live, but before he died he told Solomon to bring some sort of judgment upon him. Solomon allowed him to live at home, but he was not allowed to leave Jerusalem. Three years later, two of Shimei's servants ran away to Gath and Shimei goes after them. Solomon hears about it, calls Shimei in and reminds him that he was not supposed to leave the city, under penalty of death. He also reminds him how he had treated his father and Solomon, then has Benaiah kill Shimei, 1 Kings 2:36-46.

Soon after Solomon became king he went to Gibeon to offer sacrifice to God. God appeared to him in a dream and asked what He could give him. **Solomon praised God for the great love and care He had shown his father throughout the years and that now He had allowed David's son to sit on the throne.** Solomon says he has found himself king over such a great number of people and that he is feeling his inadequacy. He asked God to give him an understanding heart to judge his people, to discern good from evil. God was very pleased with the request of Solomon. He told Solomon since he had not asked for long life, for great wealth and power, that besides giving him the wisdom he had asked for, He would also give him great riches and honor. God also told Solomon if he would walk in His ways He would lengthen his day, 1 Kings 3:5-14.

Solomon returns to Jerusalem and it is not long until he is challenged to use the wisdom God had blessed him with. Read one of the incidents that Solomon is most famous for, from 1 Kings 3:16-28.

From 1 Kings 4:1-19, we learn how Solomon set up the governing structure of his kingdom. **Men were chosen to serve as top officials and twelve governors were selected to serve a month at a time to service the royal household.** Solomon's territory grew until it extended from the Euphrates River in the northeast to the borders of Egypt.

Then Solomon set about the task of building the temple. The work on the temple began in the fourth year of Solomon's reign, 1 Kings 6:1. **Hiram, king of Tyre**, had agreed to furnish all the wood from the cedars of Lebanon in exchange for food for his household, 1 Kings 5:1-9.

From 1 Kings 5:13 - 6:36 the building of the temple is described. It took 7 years to build. Then Solomon builds his own house which took 13 years to build, 1 Kings 7:1, and the building of it and the house for Pharaoh's daughter, whom Solomon had married, are described, verses 2-12. Also the molten sea and other vessels are made for the temple, verses 13-51. The ark was then brought up into the Most Holy Place. All Israel is gathered for the dedication of the temple.

Solomon offers a prayer of dedication, 1 Kings 8:14-61. The sacrifices for the dedication are described, verses 63-66.

God appears to Solomon the second time and said He had heard his **prayer of supplication** and tells him again that what he really has to do is to remain faithful to Him and his statutes. God repeats the promise of a perpetual kingdom to Solomon as He had to David, if Solomon will remain faithful, 1 Kings 9:1-5. God also offers some alternatives, verses 6-9.

Solomon continues to build up his empire with the slave labor of the **Canaanites**, not the Israelites, verses 20-22. With the help of Hiram he builds a navy.

Then we read another very famous incident in the life of Solomon; the visit of the **Queen of Sheba**, 1 Kings 10:1-13. Solomon's fame had reached the Queen, but after having seen the kingdom with the temple and after Solomon had answered any and all questions the Queen put to him, she told Solomon "the half had not been told," verse 7.

The riches of Solomon are brought out so vividly in the 10th chapter, I think, to set up the terrible shock of seeing that after all that God had blessed him with he throws it all away for the temporary pleasures of the world. In 1 Kings 11 we see this great king set the stage for the great and complete fall of the greatest kingdom the world had ever known. Solomon took wives of every idolatrous nation around him, something that had always been forbidden to the Israelites. He had seven hundred wives and three hundred concubines. **Thus the wisest man who had ever lived, 1 Kings 4:29-31, became a very foolish man.** He went after every god represented by his idolatrous wives; even built altars for them, 1 Kings 11:7. God became so angry with Solomon He appeared to Solomon the third and last time and told him the kingdom would be taken from him, yet for David's sake this would not be done in the days of Solomon but in the days of his son, **Rehoboam**. Only one tribe would be left to the house of David. God stirred up adversaries against Solomon for the rest of his life.

A young man named **Jeroboam** came to the attention of Solomon. Solomon notices how industrious the young man is so he makes him ruler over all the house of Joseph. If you will remember, Ephraim and Manasseh were sons of Joseph and received the inheritance of Joseph. One day as Jeroboam left the city of Jerusalem he was met by the prophet Ahijah.

Jeroboam had on a **new cloak,** and Ahijah took it and tore it into twelve pieces, and gave Jeroboam ten pieces and told him that God had said He was taking the kingdom from Solomon, leaving him one tribe for the sake of David and the city of Jerusalem; that he, Jeroboam, would reign over ten tribes. The same conditions are set forth to Jeroboam that had been given to David and Solomon, for a prosperous reign, verses 37-38. Hearing about this transaction between Ahijah and Jeroboam, Solomon tried to kill Jeroboam. Jeroboam fled down into Egypt, which will have a great bearing on his actions as king at 9 o'clock.

Solomon dies after having reigned over Israel for 40 years, verse 42. Rehoboam, Solomon's son, reigned in his stead.

Now, remember, for any added information about the life and reign of Solomon, turn and read 2 Chronicles 1-9. There are some things written there that you will want to add to your notes on Solomon.

Proverbs, Ecclesiastes, Song of Solomon

As it was suggested to read the psalms of David as you study the life of David, so it is with the writing of Solomon. **In 1 Kings 4:32 we read that Solomon wrote three thousand proverbs and one thousand and five songs.** God provides that some of Solomon's writings are preserved. Solomon wrote:

Proverbs, chapter 1:1.

Ecclesiastes, chapter 1:1 and

Song of Solomon, chapter 1:1.

As I have studied the life of Solomon to outline this portion of 8 o'clock, I have also reread Solomon's writings. **I wholeheartedly recommend that you read these books as the life of Solomon is fresh in your mind.** Only Solomon could have written Proverbs, since God had granted his wish for wisdom. God also chose the only man to write Ecclesiastes.

Just as the book of Psalms shows us the true nature of David, so these writings show us the heart of Solomon. These are important portions of the word from the mind of God and many great lessons taught from them. We should not neglect any part of God's word, for as Paul said in 2 Timothy 3:16-17, **"All scripture is given by inspiration of God, and is profitable for doctrine, for reproof, for correction, for instruction in righteousness: that the man of God may be perfect, thoroughly furnished unto all good works."** He was, at that time, speaking of the Old Testament scriptures.

The book of Job is also listed with the books of poetry. Outside the book itself, we know nothing about the author. The time for the action of the book is also uncertain. It is a book with a great lesson for us all; the lesson of relying on our faith in God under any and all circumstances.

- STUDY NOTES -

- STUDY NOTES -

- STUDY NOTES -

XII. 9 o'clock
THE DIVIDED KINGDOM

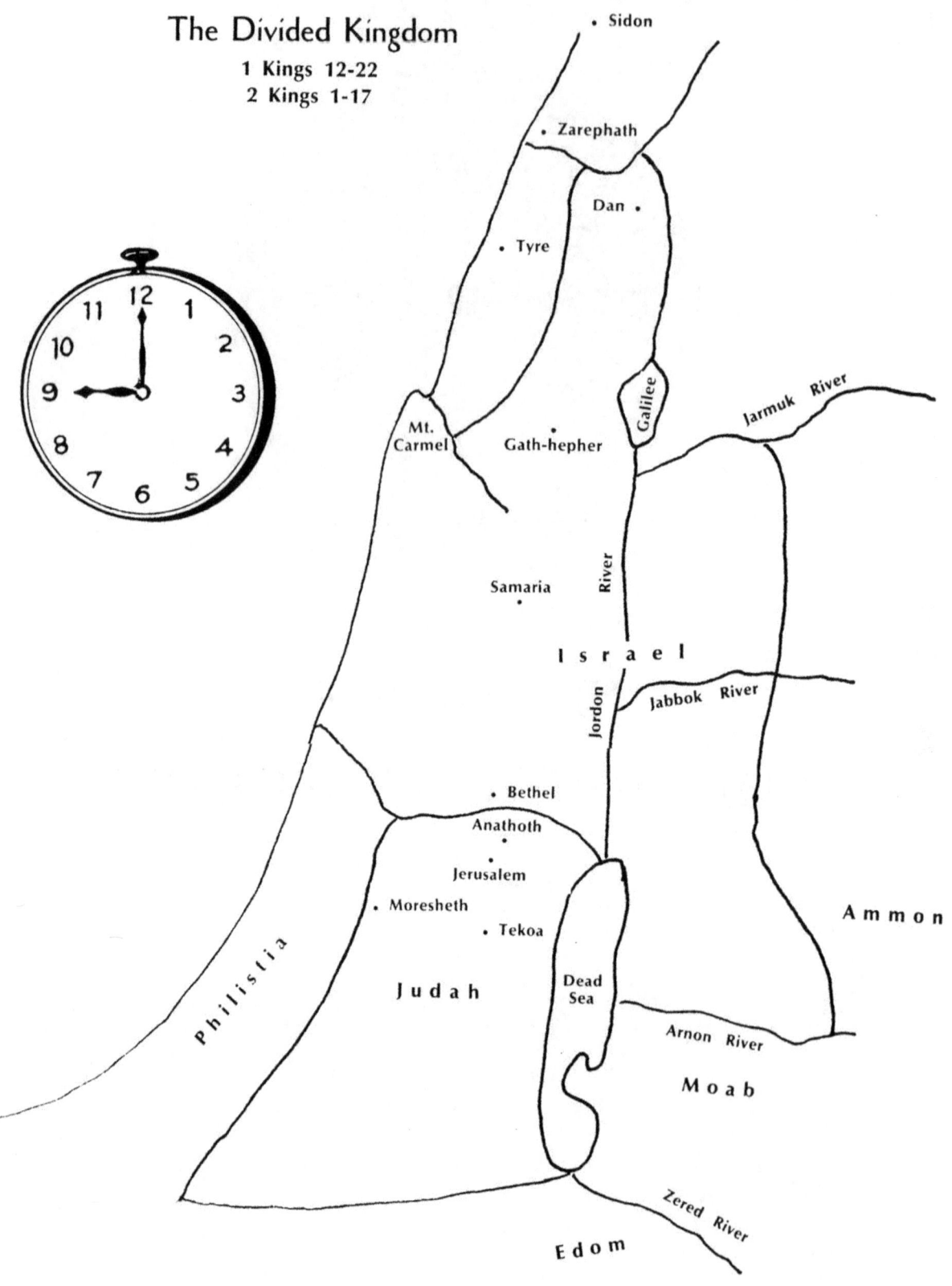

Geography

As this 9 o'clock period opens we find **two entirely separate kingdoms** of God's people. The kingdom of Israel consisted of ten tribes and the kingdom of Judah two tribes. This condition lasts for some 250 years.

Jerusalem was the capital of Judah.

Samaria was the capital of Israel.

Dan and **Bethel** were the cities where Jeroboam set up the golden calves.

Tekoa was the hometown of the prophet Amos, prophet of Israel.

Gath-hepher was the hometown of the prophet Jonah; prophet of Nineveh.

Moresheth was the hometown of the prophet Micah, prophet of Judah.

Anathoth was the hometown of the prophet Jeremiah, prophet of Judah.

The Books of Prophecy

At this time we want to bring out the fact that for this study we are going to be considering the **books of prophecy**, both major and minor, in their chronological order instead of Bible sequence. For that purpose then, we need to present this diagram of these books at this time, because the literary prophets begin to appear during this period of the Divided Kingdom. They continue to appear throughout 10, 11 and 12 o'clock, through the Restoration.

If you have always memorized the books of the Old Testament in Bible sequence, this method may be a little confusing at the out-set, but it is an understanding of the content of the book that we want to attain, and the only way to do this is to put the prophet in the correct historical background. Even though some of the things written in the prophets are for a future time, the activities of the time in which the prophet lived and wrote had a bearing on the outcome of those future events.

For the purpose, then, of better understanding the content of the books of prophecy, consider the following:

9 o'clock

Divided Kingdom	Jonah	Joel?
1 Kings 12-22	Amos	Isaiah
2 Kings 1-17	Hosea	Micah

10 o'clock

Judah Alone	Nahum	Zephaniah
2 Kings 18-23		Jeremiah
		(Lamentations)
	Obadiah?	Habakkuk

11 o'clock

Captivity		Daniel
2 Kings 24-25		Ezekiel

12 o'clock

Restoration		Haggai
1-2 Chronicles		Zechariah
Ezra, Esther, Nehemiah		Malachi

For the study of the next four periods, you will want to have in front of you the following:

a. The chart of the kings of Israel and Judah;

b. The clock with names of the prophets in their historical background;

c. Your map;

d. And most important of all, **your open Bible.**

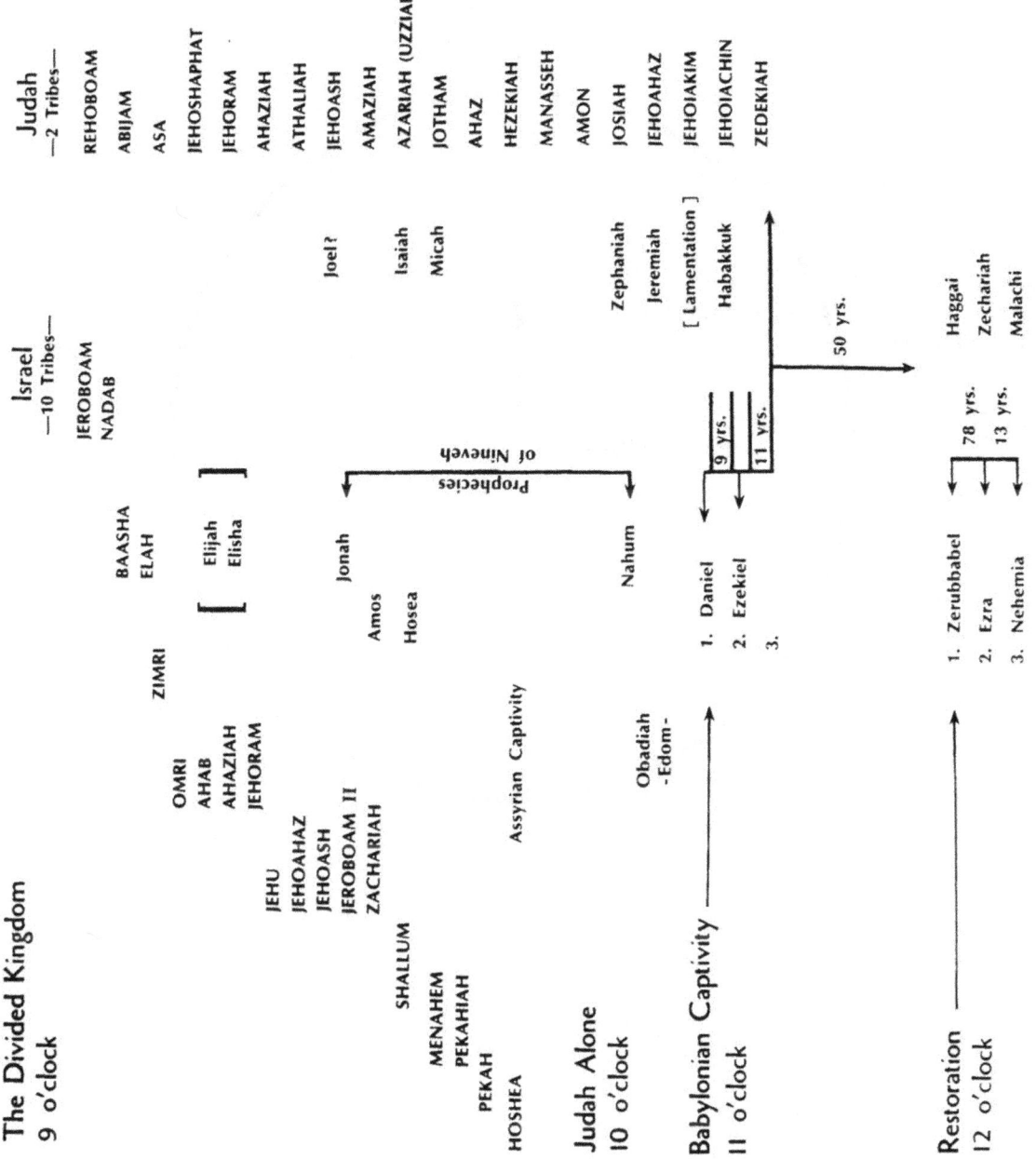

Books of Major and Minor Prophets

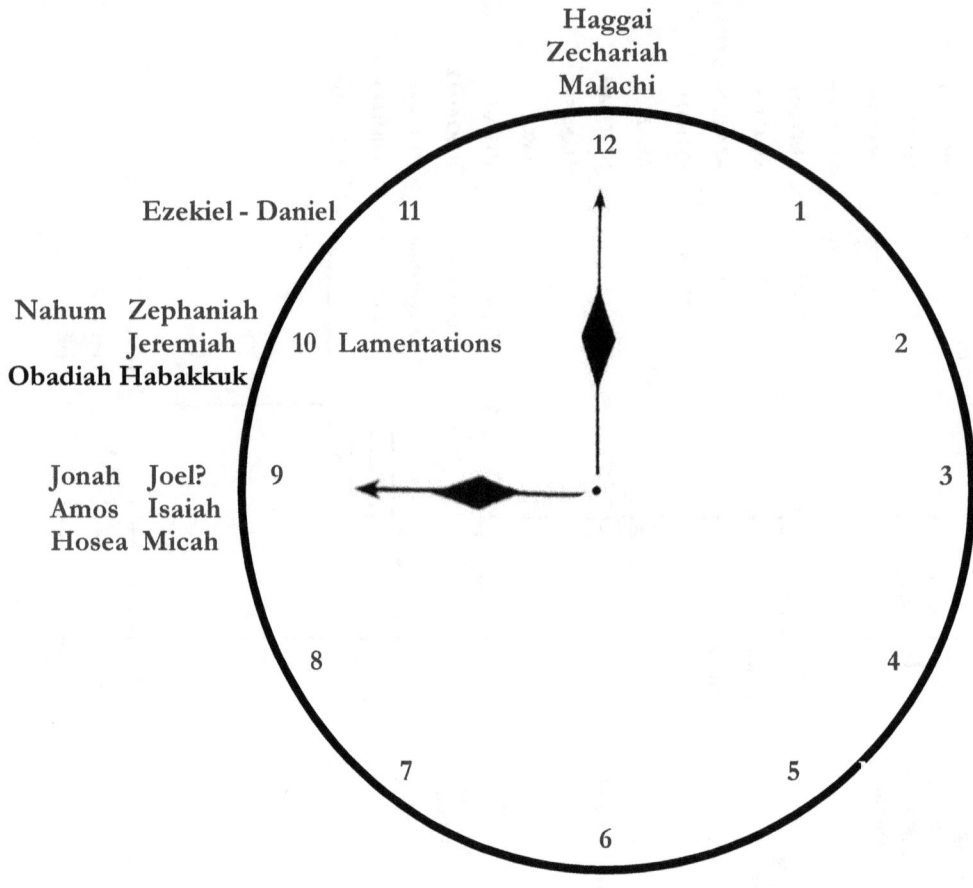

The Divided Kingdom
1 Kings 12-22
2 Kings 1-17

As this period begins, **Rehoboam**, son of Solomon, is made king over Israel at Shechem. **Jeroboam**, who is in Egypt, hears about this and returns to Israel. He goes with the people to Rehoboam and tells him that they will all serve him well if he will lighten the burdens that Solomon had laid on them in the last years of his life. Rehoboam refuses to do this, forsaking the advice of his older advisors, so the people rebel and make Jeroboam king over ten of the twelve tribes, in fulfillment of what the prophet, Ahijah, had told Jeroboam. Rehoboam reigns over Judah and Benjamin, 1 Kings 12:1-21.

There is never again a time when all the people are together under one king. We now have, for the next some two hundred and 50 years, two kingdoms. Israel, the northern kingdom, with ten tribes, with Samaria the capital city, and Judah the southern kingdom, with two tribes, with Jerusalem the capital city.

Jeroboam chooses the city of Shechem for his first capital city; later the capital will be moved to the city of Samaria. **Jeroboam, right from the very beginning, has no intentions of putting his trust in God.** He does not even want the people to continue to go to worship at the temple in Jerusalem, for fear they will turn against him. So he sets up two idols, one in **Bethel**, not more than ten miles from Jerusalem, and one in **Dan**, in the most northern part of Israel. After having been in Egypt for a time you might guess what idol Jeroboam uses: **the golden calf**. Remember when God brought Israel out of Egypt, they were encamped at Mt. Sinai and Moses had gone up to receive the ten commandment law from God. While he was up in the mountain, Aaron was leading the people in the building of the golden calf. So here we have the people ready to worship the golden calf again. They must not have had their scriptures before them or they would have known that God would not stand for such a digression. The people had been accustomed to traveling all the way down from Dan to Jerusalem for their annual sacrifices. Can you imagine them letting someone convince them that it was too far to go to Jerusalem from Bethel, only ten miles away? **From this point, for all the time the northern kingdom exists, not one king makes any effort to turn the people back to God.** Usually at the end of the life of each king of Israel, it is said, **"he walked in the way of Jeroboam, the son of Nebat, who made Israel to sin."**

For the study of the remainder of this period, consider the following outline. In 1 Kings 12-22 the kings of Judah are:

1. **Rehoboam:** 1 Kings 12:1-24; 14:21-31; 2 Chronicles 10-12. Shishak, king of Egypt invades Judah and takes all the treasures from the temple. Rehoboam **reigned for 17 years** - bad.

2. **Abijam:** 1 Kings 15:1-8; (Abijah) 2 Chronicles 13. Of Abijam it is said, "He walked in all the sins of his father .... and his heart was not perfect with the Lord his God, as the heart of David his father." Abijam **reigned 3 years** - bad.

3. **Asa:** 1 Kings 15:9-24; 2 Chronicles 14-16. Asa was one of only about four of the kings of Judah who tried to turn the tide of idolatry among the people. He **reigned 41 years** - good.

4. **Jehoshaphat:** 1 Kings 22:1-50; 2 Chronicles 17-20. Jehoshaphat "walked in all the ways of Asa his father; .... doing that which was right in the eyes of the Lord; Nevertheless the high places were not taken down." Jehoshaphat **reigned 25 years** - good.

In the southern kingdom of Judah the son followed his father on the throne, but in Israel there were nine different families represented on the throne. These families will be called dynasties.

So for 1 Kings 12-22 the kings of Israel are:

1st Dynasty:

Jeroboam, 1 Kings 12:12 - 14:20. Established idolatry; "Made Israel to sin." Jeroboam **reigned for 22 years** - bad.

Nadab, 1 Kings 15:25-28. Slain by Baasha after **reigning for 2 years** - bad.

2nd Dynasty:

Baasha, 1 Kings 15:27-16:7. Baasha killed all of Jeroboam's family. Baasha moved the capital to Tirzah. He **reigned 24 years** - bad.

Elah, 1 Kings 16:8-14. Elah was slain in Tirzah by Zimri. He **reigned 2 years** - bad.

3rd Dynasty:

Zimri, 1 Kings 16:15-20. Upon hearing that Zimri had killed the king, the people make Omri, the captain of the army, king. Omri went up against the city of Tirzah and when Zimri learned of Omri's plans he burned his house down around him and died. Zimri **reigned one week** - bad.

4th Dynasty:

Omri, 1 Kings 16:16-28. Omri moves the capital to Samaria. He **reigned 12 years** - bad.

Ahab, 1 Kings 16:29 - 22:40. Of all the kings of Israel, during the divided kingdom, I suppose Ahab is the most familiar to most people. With the influence of his wife, Jezebel, he brings the people down to a new low in idolatry. Elijah, the prophet, appears during Ahab's reign. Ahab **reigned 22 years** - bad.

Ahaziah, 1 Kings 22:50-53; 2 Kings 1:1-18. In trying to capture Elijah, two companies of men with their captains, sent by Ahaziah, were consumed by fire from heaven. Ahaziah **reigned two 2 years** - very bad.

These are the kings of Judah and Israel recorded in 1 Kings 12-22-2 Kings 1. In 2 Kings 2 the translation of Elijah is recorded. We then go into the labors of Elisha. Both of these prophets are associated with the kings of Israel. 2 Kings opens with the reigns of the kings of Israel. The fourth dynasty continues:

Jehoram, 2 Kings 1:17-9:26. The translation of Elijah. The remainder of these chapters have mostly to do with the life of Elisha. Jehoram **reigned 12 years** - bad.

5th Dynasty:

Jehu, 2 Kings 9:1-10:1-36. Jehu destroys all of the house of Ahab, Jezebel also. He also destroys all the prophets of Baal along with the images out of the house of Baal, and last of all the image of Baal. This was all good, but he still held to the worship that Jeroboam had instituted, that of the golden calf. At this time we see that God is beginning to cut away at the northern kingdom, in the taking of the eastern side of the Jordan by the Syrians. Jehu **reigned 28 years**; bad.

Jehoahaz, 2 Kings 13:1-9. Jehoahaz followed in the footsteps of Jeroboam. God was angry with Israel and brought the people under the oppression of Hazael, king of Syria and his son, Benhadad. Jehoahaz prayed to God, and God lifted the oppression. However, this doesn't make the impression on Jehoahaz that God would have liked. Jehoahaz did not depart from the sins of Jeroboam, who made Israel sin. Jehoahaz **reigned 17 years** - bad.

Jehoash, 2 Kings 13:10 - 14:16. Elisha dies in chapter 13. Jehoash went up to Jerusalem, broke down part of the walls and took the vessels of gold and silver from the temple and palace. Jehoash **reigned 16 years** - bad.

Jeroboam II, 2 Kings 14:23-29. The literary prophets now begin to appear. Jonah told Jeroboam II that he would be victorious over the Syrians. So this is the background for the things of the book of Jonah. God has a purpose for saving the capital city of Assyria, Nineveh, at the preaching of Jonah. We will see later how He uses the Assyrians against Israel. The prophets Amos and Hosea begin their work in the reign of Jeroboam II; Amos 1:1 and Hosea 1:1. You will want to keep this in mind as you study these two books. Jeroboam II **reigned 14 years** - bad.

Zachariah, 2 Kings 15:8-12. Zachariah had **reigned only 6 months** when Shallum killed him and seized the throne. God had told Jehu his sons would reign until the fourth generation - bad.

6th Dynasty:

Shallum, 2 Kings 15:13-15. Shallum **reigned one month** and was killed by Menahem - bad.

7th Dynasty

Menahem, 2 Kings 15:16-22. There was none more cruel than this man to attain his goals. Pul, or Tiglath-pilezer, as he is better known, king of Assyria, attempts to invade Israel. Menahem pays him off but only postpones the invasion. Menahem **reigned 10 years** - terrible.

Pekahiah, 2 Kings 15:23-26. Pekahiah "departed not from the sins of Jeroboam, son of Nebat, who made Israel to sin." He was killed by one of his captains, Pekah. Pekahiah **reigned 2 years** - bad.

8th Dynasty:

Pekah, 2 Kings 15:27-31. Tiglath-pilezer, king of Assyria, invades Israel, but this time he captures a lot of territory and takes many captives to Assyria. Pekah "departed not from the sins of Jeroboam, son of Nebat, who made Israel to sin." Pekah **reigned 20 years** - bad.

9th Dynasty:

Hoshea, 2 Kings 17:1-23. Shalmaneser seized the throne of Assyria. He invaded Israel, but while besieging Samaria he died. Sargon usurped the throne of Assyria and all of Israel, the northern kingdom, crumbled. The ten tribes are captured and most of the people scattered throughout the lands taken by Assyria. This was the purpose for which Nineveh was given an opportunity to repent to the preaching of Jonah. The prophet Hosea is the second and last literary prophet for Israel, the northern kingdom. He is called "the weeping prophet of Israel." It would be well to read that book now, in that the historical background of the book is fresh in your mind. Hoshea **reigned 9 years** - bad.

We find in 2 Kings 17:7-18 the reasons for the total destruction of the kingdom of Israel. God said, through the prophet Hosea in Hosea 4:6, **"My people are destroyed for lack of knowledge: because thou hast rejected knowledge, I will reject thee, that thou shalt be no priest to me: seeing thou hast forgotten the law of thy God, I will also forget thy children."**

We have gone through the dynasties of Israel, now let's go back to 2 Kings 8 and continue with the kings of Judah who reigned during the divided kingdom.

5. **Jehoram**, 2 Kings 8:16-24; 2 Chronicles 21. Jehoram married the daughter of Ahab and Jezebel. He allowed his wife, Athaliah, to influence him, as Jezebel influenced Ahab. He walked in the ways of the kings of Israel. We will find Athaliah every bit the wicked woman her mother was. Jehoram **reigned 8 years** - bad.

6. **Ahaziah**, 2 Kings 8:25 - 9:29; 2 Chronicles 22:1-9. Ahaziah was the son of Jehoram and Athaliah. He allied himself with Jehoram, king of Israel, against Hazael, king of Syria. Jehoram is wounded and he goes to Jezreel to recover from his wounds. Ahaziah, king of Judah, had gone up to visit him when by the help of Elisha, Jehu is made king over Israel. Jehu comes to Jezreel and slays Jehoram of

Israel and also Ahaziah of Judah. Ahaziah **reigned one year** - bad.

7. **Athaliah,** 2 Kings 11:1-20; 2 Chronicles 22:10-23:15. This is one of the three times that a son did not follow his father on the throne. When Athaliah heard that her son was dead she went about to kill all her grandsons to gain the throne. However, her daughter, Jehosheba, took Joash, son of Ahaziah and hid him in the temple. He was just 2 years old when Athaliah seized the throne. He remained hidden in the temple for 6 years. When the time was right, Jehoiada, the priest, had the temple surrounded by guards and brought Joash forward and crowned him king. Athaliah was then put to death. Athaliah **reigned 6 years** - terrible.

8. **Jehoash,** 2 Kings 12:1-21; (Joash) 2 Chronicles 23-24. Jehoash was seven years old when he became king. He had been trained by Jehoiada the priest. He made every effort to restore the temple and to turn the hearts of the people back to God. He is one of the four or five kings of Judah who tried to be a good king. Hazael, king of Syria, came against Jerusalem, and Joash gathered all the gold he could find and gave it to Hazael. Then he withdrew from Jerusalem. Two of the servants of Joash kill him. Jehoash **reigned 40 years** - good.

9. **Amaziah,** 2 Kings 14:1-20; 2 Chronicles 25. The first thing Amaziah does as king is to slay the servants who had slain his father. He also defeated the Edomites in battle. He then invites Jehoash, king of Israel, to meet him in battle. Jehoash tries to get Amaziah to be satisfied with his victory over the Edomites. Amaziah insists, so he goes against Jehoash and is defeated. This is when Jehoash destroys part of the walls of Jerusalem and takes all the gold and silver and treasures from the temple and palace, as well as captives, back to Samaria. Amaziah was not a bad king, but he did not destroy the idols. Amaziah **reigned 29 years** - good?

10. **Azariah,** 2 Kings 14:21-22; 15:1-7; (Uzziah) 2 Chronicles 26. Azariah is called Uzziah in 2 Chronicles, and also in Isaiah 1:1. So it is during the reign of this king and the next three kings that Isaiah labored. Azariah's downfall was going into the temple to burn incense. He was struck with leprosy for the rest of his life and his son Jotham ruled in his stead; any lepers had to be isolated from the rest of the people. Azariah **reigned 52 years** - good?

11. **Jotham,** 2 Kings 15:32-38; 2 Chronicles 27. The prophet Micah wrote in Micah 1:1 that it was during the reign of Jotham, Ahaz, and Hezekiah that the word of the Lord came to him. Jotham **reigned 16 years** - good?

12. **Ahaz,** 2 Kings 16:1-20; 2 Chronicles 28. Thus far Ahaz is the worst king Judah has known. You would think he was a king of Israel. No king of Israel followed more closely to the ways of Jeroboam than did Ahaz of Judah. Notice, here again we see the rise of the Assyrians who are about to destroy Israel. Ahaz **reigned 16 years** - terrible.

13. **Hezekiah,** 2 Kings 18:1-20:21; 2 Chronicles 29-32. There is more recorded of the life of King Hezekiah than any other king of Judah, as with Ahab of Israel. He is one of only two of whom it is said, **"He did that which was right in the sight of God, according to all that David his father did."** Read 18:3-6. Hezekiah came to the throne in the third year of the last king of Israel, Hoshea. It was in the ninth year of the reign of Hoshea, sixth of the reign of Hezekiah, that Israel was taken into Assyrian captivity, never again to be restored, the so-called lost ten tribes of Israel. The period of the two kingdoms, the divided kingdom, comes to an end. Only Judah is left.

The lives of the prophets **Elijah** and **Elisha** are so much a part of this period of the Old Testament. You will want to isolate the life of each one of them and make your notes on their activities. Any Old Testament student is expected to know these two men very well. They are the best known of any of the prophets, excepting the literary prophets. Elijah, 1 Kings 17:1-2 Kings 2:11; Malachi 4:5-6; Matthew 17:4; Luke 1:17. Elisha, 1 Kings 19:16 - 2 Kings 13:21.

Before we leave this 9 o'clock period, let's look again at the clock of the books of prophecy provided in this section.

Notice that this system is providing each one of us a mental concordance of the books of the Old Testament. For instance, having already learned that the historical background for 9 o'clock is 1 Kings 12-22 - 2 Kings 1-17, you will want to know if the Bible has any other information concerning this period. You can look at this clock and readily see that it does. This information is as follows:

9 o'clock

Divided Kingdom	Jonah	Joel?
1 Kings 12-22	Amos	Isaiah
2 Kings 1-17	Hosea	Micah

There is a question mark at the name of Joel only because we do not know exactly when he lived and wrote. However, in the book of Joel are some of the most important prophecies written concerning what was to follow the establishment of the church. Read Joel 2:28-32 in preparation for the study of Acts 2 in the New Testament. A lot of the problems of the gift of the Holy Spirit can be eliminated with this preparation.

- STUDY NOTES -

- STUDY NOTES -

STUDY NOTES

XIII. 10 o'clock
JUDAH ALONE

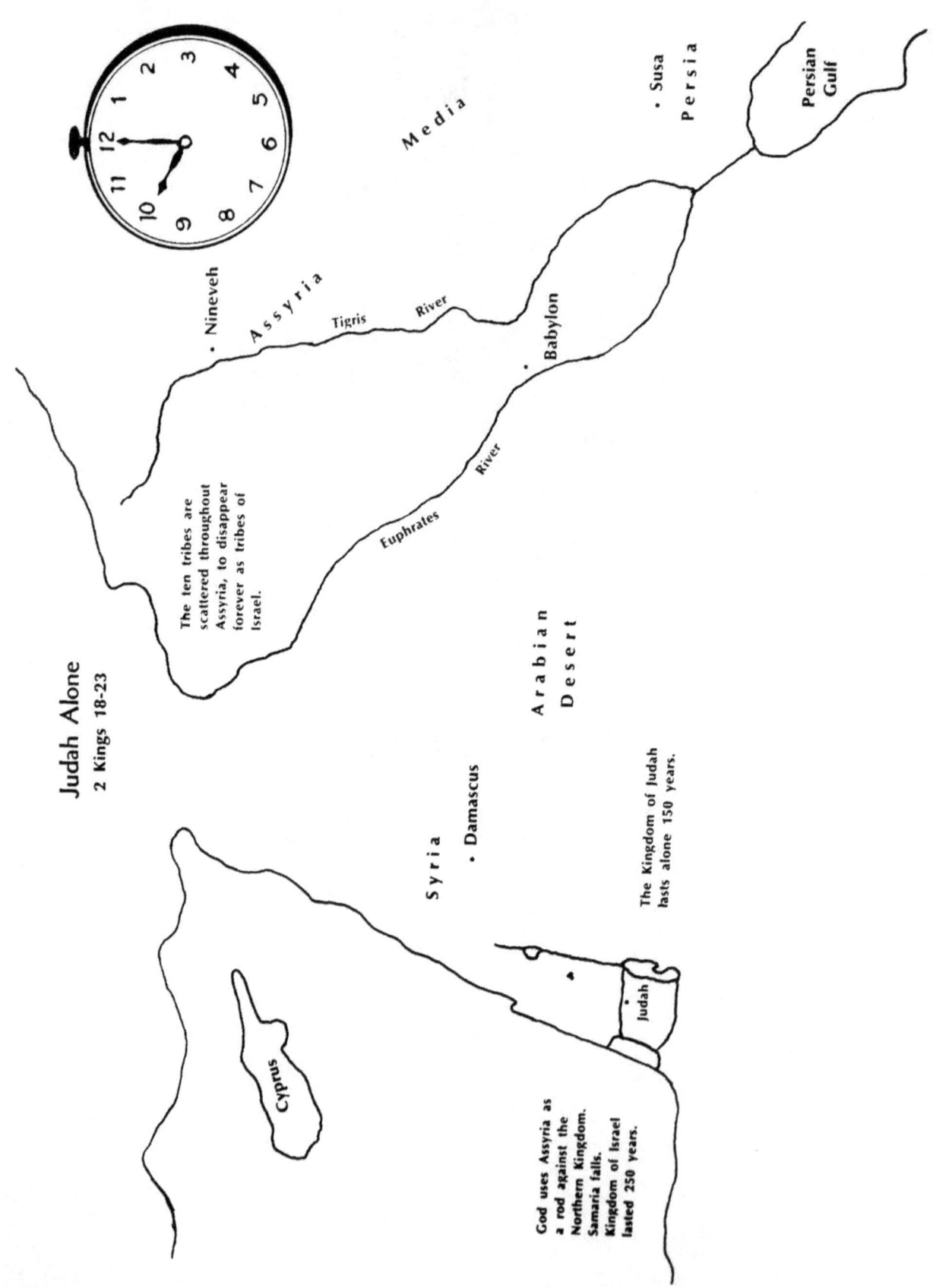

Judah Alone
2 Kings 18-23

For this period we continue with the life of King Hezekiah. Remember that the kingdom of Israel is gone. Shalmaneser was the king of Assyria who took the ten tribes captive in the sixth year of the reign of King Hezekiah of Judah. These people, as tribes or as a kingdom, disappear from the pages of history. The reason being that the people had so inter-married that Israel lost its identity.

By the fourteenth year of King Hezekiah, Sennacherib is king of Assyria. It is he who taunts Hezekiah and the people.

13. **Hezekiah,** 2 Kings 18:1 - 20:21; 2 Chronicles 29-32. The greatest revival since David and Solomon takes place during the reign of Hezekiah. He sets up the temple and sanctifies it as thoroughly as did Solomon when he built it. He invites those people who are left in the lands of the northern tribes to come to Jerusalem and participate, which some of them do. Hezekiah calls on Isaiah for assistance in laying their problems with Assyria before God. God takes care of Assyria. Assyria's power is broken. When Hezekiah had been healed of a sickness and God added 15 years to his life, the son of the king of a faraway land, Babylon, sent messengers with letters and a present, having heard that he was ill. While the messengers were in Jerusalem, Hezekiah showed them all the treasures of his kingdom. Isaiah came to Hezekiah and asked him who the men were and what they saw in Jerusalem. Hezekiah told Isaiah they were from Babylon and Isaiah tells him of the future captivity of Judah by Babylon. Hezekiah **reigned 29 years** - one of the best.

14. **Manasseh,** 2 Kings 21:1-18; 2 Chronicles 33:1-20. Judah hits a new low under Manasseh. You just can't imagine this being the son of the greatest reformer Judah had known. He reversed all the good his father had accomplished, and it is said that all the nations around Judah could not have influenced the people into such degradation as did Manasseh. He was finally brought down by the Assyrians and then was taken as a prisoner to Babylon. He repents and prays to God, and God restores him to Jerusalem. He tries to undo all the wrong he had brought on Judah. Manasseh **reigned 55 years** - terrible.

15. **Amon,** 2 Kings 21:19-26; 2 Chronicles 33:21-25. Amon lived and ruled as his father had, except he never repented of his wickedness. He was slain by his servants. The people slay the servants and make Josiah, son of Amon, king. Amon **reigned 2 years** - bad.

16. **Josiah,** 2 Kings 22:1 - 23:30; 2 Chronicles 34-35. Josiah is the second and last of the great reformers of the period of Judah Alone. He did as Hezekiah had done. He restored the temple with its worship and tore down every sign of idolatry in the land. The book of the law was found in the temple, and Josiah read and adhered to it for the restoration of allegiance to God. It was during the reign of Josiah that the prophets Zephaniah and Jeremiah labored and wrote Zephaniah 1:1 and Jeremiah 1:2. Josiah **reigned 31 years** - one of the best.

We notice also that during the reign of Josiah, Egypt goes against the Assyrians at Charchemish. Josiah goes against Egypt and is killed at Megiddo. Later, both Egypt and Assyria are defeated by Babylon. It is the downfall of Assyria, with its capital city of Nineveh, that is the subject of the book of Nahum. Nineveh is saved in the book of Jonah, but its fall is at hand in the book of Nahum. There is no contradiction in the books, it is just a matter of knowing when the two books fit in the history of the Old Testament, 150 years apart.

17. **Jehoahaz,** 2 Kings 23:31-34; 2 Chronicles 36:1-4. Jehoahaz had only reigned three months when Necho, Pharaoh of Egypt, put Judah under tribute, took Jehoahaz to Egypt and put his brother, Jehoiakim, on

the throne. Jehoahaz **reigned three months** - bad.

It is at this time that Egyptian and Assyrian powers are both broken entirely by the Babylonians. As Nahum's prophecies concerned the overthrow of the Assyrians, Habakkuk's prophecies are concerned with the Babylonian Captivity, and the eventual overthrow of the Babylonians, or Chaldeans, as they are also called. Jeremiah and Habakkuk live to see the complete and total destruction of Judah. Jeremiah's writings in the book of Lamentations has to do with Jerusalem's fall.

As at the end of 9 o'clock, the Divided Kingdom, we noticed how we can have a mental concordance of the books of the Old Testament. Let's look now at 10 o'clock and make the same application. On the clock of the prophets notice that when you have studied 2 Kings 18-23, you have studied the historical background for the prophecies of:

10 o'clock

Judah Alone	Nahum	Zephaniah
2 Kings 18-23		Jeremiah
		(Lamentations)

Obadiah (Edom?) Habakkuk

Remember the Edomites, the descendants of Esau? Obadiah, in his book, talks about how the Edomites rejoiced over the way the descendants of Jacob have been brought down. Because of their exultation over the sad state of Judah God says He will destroy them as a nation, no matter how secure they think they are against an invasion. They are to receive what Judah has received, except that Judah will be restored and Edom will not.

- STUDY NOTES -

- STUDY NOTES -

XIV. 11 o'clock
CAPTIVITY

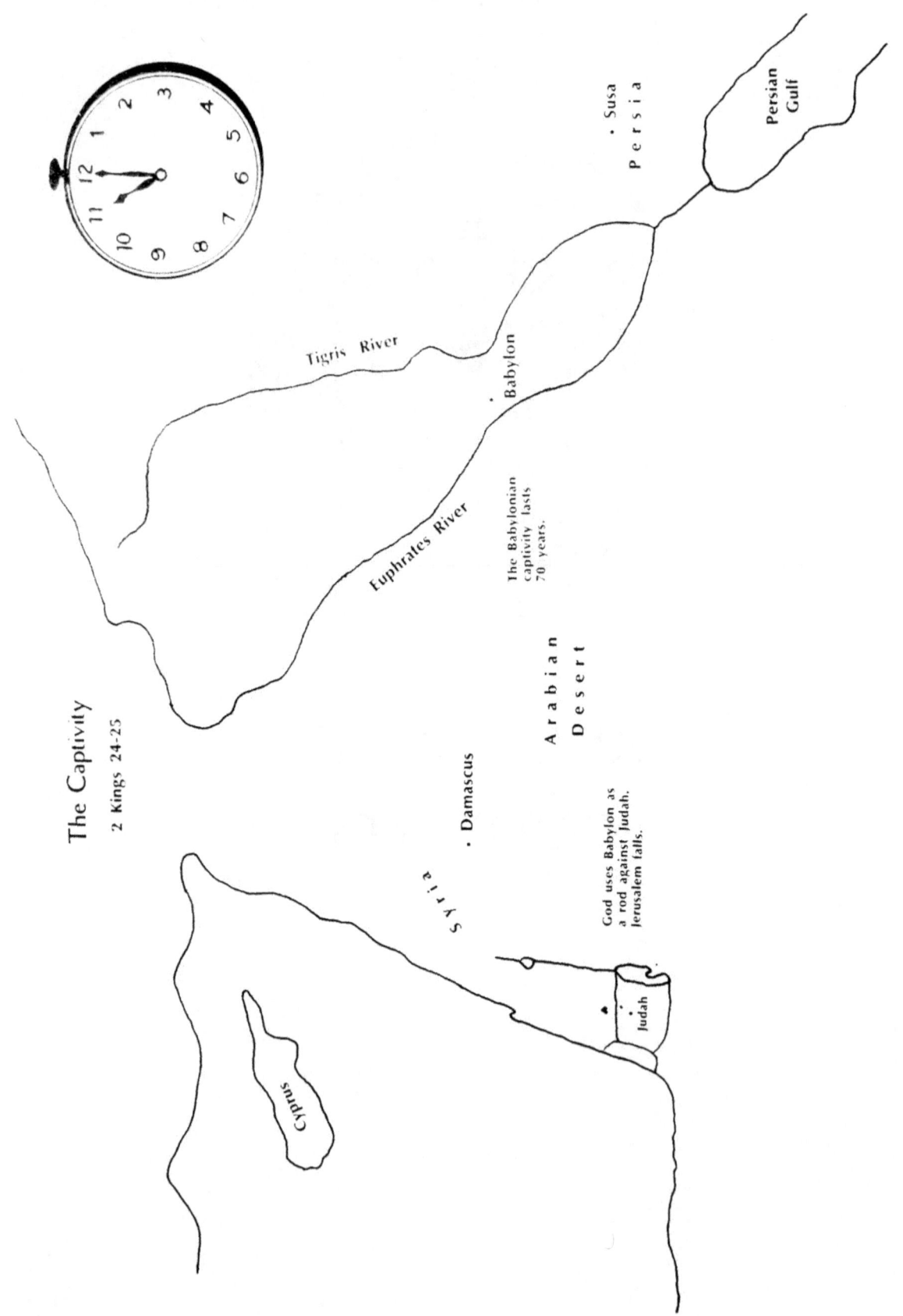

The Babylonian Captivity
2 Kings 24-25

The Babylonian Captivity began in the reign of Jehoiakim. The power of the Assyrians is a thing of the past. The Babylonians are becoming the world power. God uses the Babylonians as a rod against Judah as He used the Assyrians against Israel. The difference being that there is to be a restoration of Judah. Along with the bad news of captivities, by the prophets, there is also the good news of a restoration. Isaiah even calls Cyrus by name as the one who is to allow the restoration to begin, Isaiah 44:28, many years before the Persian Empire is even thought of.

18. **Jehoiakim,** 2 Kings 23:34 - 24:6; 2 Chronicles 36: 4-8. It was during the reign of Jehoiakim that Nebuchadnezzar, king of Babylon, begins his siege of Jerusalem. Nebuchadnezzar carried the treasures of the temple to Babylon, along with many captives, including the young man Daniel, who is later called to be a prophet. Jehoiakim became a puppet king for the king of Babylon. He dies and is buried outside the walls of Jerusalem. Jehoiakim **reigned 11 years** - bad.

19. **Jehoiachin,** 2 Kings 24:8-16; 2 Chronicles 36:9-10. The second stage of the Babylonian Captivity takes place 11 years after the first stage and three months after Jehoiachin becomes king. He, along with the entire royal family, and with anyone else of any consequence, is taken to Babylon. This is the time that Ezekiel is taken. Ezekiel is later called to be a prophet among the people. Jehoiachin is imprisoned, but after 37 years was released. Jehoiachin is called Jeconiah in the book of Jeremiah. Jehoiachin **reigned three months** - bad.

20. **Zedekiah,** 2 Kings 24:18 - 25:21; 2 Chronicles 36. 11-20. Zedekiah was also son of Josiah, as were Jehoahaz and Jehoiakim. He is the last king to reign over Judah. Nebuchadnezzar comes over and totally destroys the city of Jerusalem. The temple is torn down completely as are the walls of Jerusalem. Zedekiah's sons are murdered before his eyes, and then his eyes are put out and he is taken in chains to Babylon. The priests are killed along with those in charge of the army. Gedaliah is made governor over what was left of the people, and he is killed. The once great kingdom of Judah is desolated.

The Babylonian Captivity has been in progress for 20 years by this time. It will take another 50 years to fulfill the 70 years that Jeremiah talks about in Jeremiah 29:10; also read Daniel 9:2.

Now, as you will notice, 2 Kings ends with the people in captivity, whereas the last two verses of 2 Chronicles tell of the restoration under Cyrus, king of Persia. So we can see that the Chronicles were compiled at 12 o'clock, after the decree of Cyrus had been issued and some of the people had returned to Jerusalem.

It is at this time that the books of Ezekiel and Daniel are to be examined. Even though they contain an abundance of figurative language you can, by reading them, see where they fit historically.

Then for that mental concordance notice on the clock of the prophets where Ezekiel and Daniel appear:

11 o'clock

Captivity	Ezekiel
2 Kings 24-25	Daniel

The prophecy of Daniel begins from about the third year of his own captivity and extends throughout the Babylonian Captivity and into the Persian Empire. Ezekiel's prophecy begins with the fifth year of his own captivity and extends into the Babylonian Captivity about 16 years. So you can see that these two men were at work with the captives in Babylon at the same time Jeremiah and

Habakkuk were at work among the people in Jerusalem. It is to Ezekiel and Daniel that we turn to get any information that is available to us for the fifty years between the final destruction of Jerusalem and the end of the Babylonian Captivity.

- STUDY NOTES -

- STUDY NOTES -

XV. 12 o'clock
RESTORATION

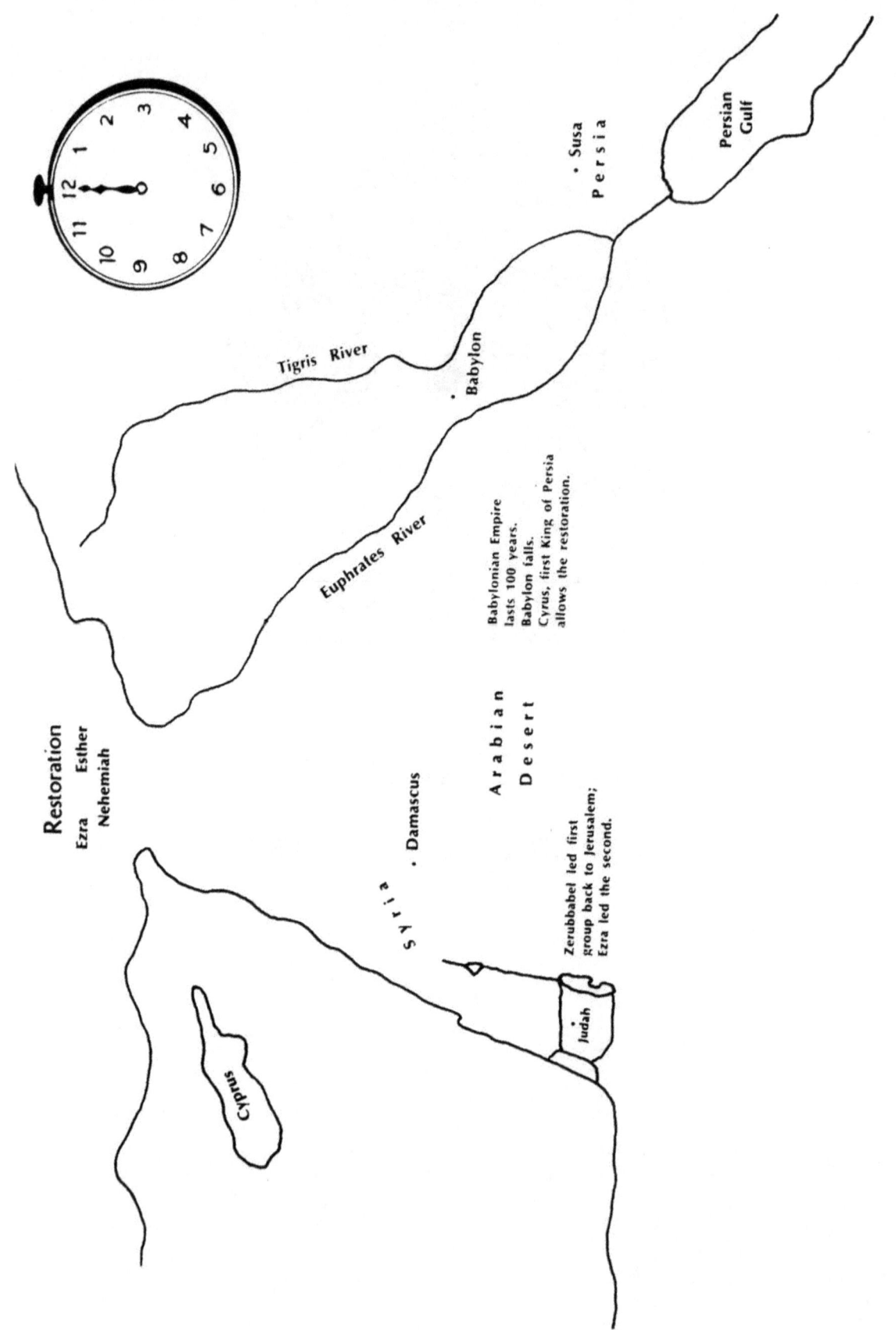

Restoration

Ezra 1-6; Esther
Ezra 7-10; Nehemiah

The first three verses of Ezra contain the same words as the last two verses of 2 Chronicles. Thus we can see that we are entering the period of the **Restoration**.

Some 200 years earlier, before the Persian Empire was even thought of, Isaiah, in talking about the restoration, even goes so far as to calling the man by name who would allow the restoration to get underway. In Isaiah 44:29; 45:1 the man is called **Cyrus**. Isaiah talks about this man rebuilding the temple in a time when the temple still stood, and it continued to stand for another 100 years or so. It was hard for the people to pay attention to men who were saying their great nation would fall and that their temple would be destroyed and have to be rebuilt. **It seems that only the people close to God, those who looked to Him for instruction and guidance, could see the awful things coming that the inspired prophets were talking about.** There was always a remnant of the people who maintained their faith and trust in God, even when their leaders were not providing conditions under which they could function adequately in their worship to Him. I know it must have grieved God to have the faithful suffer along with the guilty, but He had to purge, once and for all, idolatry from among His people. **As we look ahead we will find that God's way is the way.** After the Babylonian Captivity, and since that day, the Jews have been free from the sin of idolatry.

For a good understanding of the Restoration Period, we need to think of it happening in three, separate stages. If you will remember, at 9 o'clock, there is a clock which shows the chronological order of the prophets. At 12 o'clock the prophets are Haggai, Zechariah and Malachi. So for the study of the first stage of the restoration, Ezra 1-6 should be read, along with the books of Haggai and Zechariah.

The book of Esther will interrupt the restoration and should be read after Ezra 6. To understand why we do this, look at Ezra 6 and see that **the king of Persia is Darius**, who is the third king, after Cyrus and Cambyses. Then notice in Ezra 7 **the king of Persia is Artaxerxes**. This Artaxerxes is the son of Ahasuerus or Xerxes, husband of Esther; and he is the fifth king of Persia.

For the study of **the second stage of the restoration**, then, we need to read Ezra 7-10, and the books of Nehemiah and Malachi for the last stage.

In Ezra 1-6 we have a period of about 20 years. **Zerubbabel** is the one who leads that first group back to Jerusalem, Ezra 2:2. He is also made governor, Haggai 2:2. Zerubbabel was the grandson of King Jehoiachin, I Chronicles 3:17; Ezra 3:8. Remember that Jehoiachin is also Jeconiah, 1 Chronicles 3:16; also see 2 Kings 24:6. Therefore Zerubbabel is a descendant of Jesus; see also Matthew 1:12; Luke 3:27.

Since the temple would require years to rebuild, and yet the immediate need was to get the attention of the people on the worship to God according to the Law of Moses, **the altar of burnt offering was erected**. They proceeded also to celebrate the feast days as laid down in the Law of Moses.

Then in the second year after the return to Jerusalem, Zerubbabel, along with Jeshua, the high priest, lead the people in the attempt to rebuild the temple. **The foundation is laid, and there the work stops for another 15 years.** In Ezra 4 we see that they were hindered from finishing the temple throughout the reign of Cyrus, even to the reign of Darius, verse 5, who was the third king of Persia. **It was at the time of Darius that Haggai and Zechariah, the prophets, stir up the people once again to finish the temple.** A letter is sent to King Darius, asking that he search for the decree of Cyrus allowing the people to return to Jerusalem to rebuild the temple. The decree is found and the building of the temple is resumed. **It took 4 years to finish the temple, Ezra 4:24; 6:15.**

It takes the reading of the book of **Haggai** to see the attitude of the people toward their finishing of the temple during the fifteen year lapse after laying the foundation. It seems that with a little adversity they simply turned their hearts and minds to their own homes and comforts. **In less than a month, however, Haggai had them all excited again and the work did not stop until the temple was finished.** Haggai may not have seen the temple finished. Zechariah takes over where Haggai leaves off, in encouraging the people.

You might want to notice that it is from the time of the restoration that the children of Israel are called Jews. Originally the name "Jew" meant "those of the kingdom of Judah". Later, however, the name came to mean any who was a descendant of Abraham.

Esther

The events of the book of Esther take place some 33 years after the temple is completed and some 16 years before the events of Ezra 7-10. You will find as you read this book that God's name is not once mentioned.

From Esther 1:1 we can see just how far the **Persian Empire** extended. It extended from India in the east to Ethiopia in the south-west. However, it also extended through Asia in the northwest. So we need to understand that the danger to the Jews, presented in the book, extended throughout the Persian Empire, and not just in the proximity of **Susa**, the capital city and the immediate scene of the events of the book.

Ahasuerus reigns on the Persian throne at this time. He is also known by historians as Xerxes. He has a beautiful wife named Vashti, Esther 1:11. He had commanded that she come before him and his princes and nobles during a feast, so he could show off his beautiful wife. Vashti refused to obey the commandment and, on the advice of the king's lawyers, was removed from being queen of Persia, verse 19. A law was then made throughout the empire that the man was to be ruler in his own home, verse 22.

Then a search is begun to find a new queen, Esther 2. In the palace there was a Jew named **Mordecai**. He had a young cousin whom he had raised as his daughter, since the death of her parents. **Her name in Hebrew was Hadassah and in the Greek it was Esther, which means "a star."** Esther was among the young maidens who were brought to the palace for the purpose of allowing the king to make his choice for a queen. Esther is chosen by Ahasuerus and she becomes the queen of Persia. Mordecai has persuaded her not to reveal the fact that she is a Jew.

In verses 21-23 there is an event that later plays a part in helping the position of the Jews. Mordecai saves the king from assassination by two chamberlains. Mordecai tells Esther of the plot, Esther tells Ahasuerus and the two chamberlains are hanged. The incident is then recorded in the chronicles of the kings of Persia.

Also in the palace was a prince named **Haman**. Ahasuerus promotes Haman above all the other princes, and commands that all the servants of the palace bow to Haman. All of them did except Mordecai. **Haman was told that there was a Jew in the palace who would not show him reverence.** This makes Haman furious and he is not satisfied with the idea of taking care of just Mordecai, he wants to eliminate all the Jews throughout the Persian Empire. Lots are cast as to what day this is to take place. Haman even gets permission from the king and a decree is written and sent throughout the empire that in the twelfth month, on the thirteenth day, every Jew, both young and old, children and women, would be killed, Esther 3.

When the decree was sent out, Mordecai and all the Jews wept bitterly. **Esther is told by Mordecai that she and she alone can save her people from the plot of Haman.** She, of course, knows that she takes her life in her hands if she approaches the king if he has not sent for her. Mordecai then reminds her that she, being a Jew, would die anyway if

Haman's plans are carried out. He also puts it this way, **"Who knoweth whether thou art come to the kingdom for such a time as this?"**

Accepting her responsibilities, Esther seems to be very patient about choosing just the right time to tell her husband what **Haman** is planning for her people. She was granted an audience with the king. She invites the king and Haman to a banquet. Haman is very happy to be invited to the queen's banquet, but his happiness is short lived when he goes out and **Mordecai** won't bow down to him.

When Haman goes home that night after the banquet he tells his wife and his friends how great are his riches and how the king has promoted him above all the other princes, and how he was the only other man at **Queen Esther's banquet,** and was also invited to another one the next day. Yet all of this gave him no pleasure as long as Mordecai was allowed to be in the king's court. So his wife suggests that he hang Mordecai. The gallows Haman built that very night were about eighty feet high, Esther 5:1-14.

That night the king is unable to sleep and he calls for the chronicles to read. **He reads the record of the attempt on his life and asks if Mordecai had ever been honored in any way for having saved his life.** He was told that nothing had been done for Mordecai. Haman, in the meantime, has come into the outer court, hoping to see the king to get permission to hang Mordecai. **Ahasuerus** calls him in. He asks Haman what should be done to someone the king wants to honor. Thinking that it was he who was to be honored, he said the man should be treated like a king, Esther 6:8-9. Can you imagine Haman's shock and humiliation in having Mordecai honored in such a way, and that he himself, has to do the honors, verse 11?

That night at Esther's second banquet she reveals to her husband the plot of Haman against her and her people, explaining to him that she is a Jew and Mordecai's daughter, Esther 8:1. Haman is then hanged on the gallows he had built for Mordecai, Esther 7:10.

The decree that the king had sent out for the destruction of the Jews could not be rescinded, but Ahasuerus allowed Mordecai to send out another decree that allowed the Jews to protect themselves, Esther 8:11. Mordecai also sends out letters to all the Jews that this deliverance will be celebrated annually on the thirteenth and fourteenth days of the twelfth month of Adar. **The feast day will be called Purim**, from the word Pur, read Esther 3:7; 9:24, 26.

To this day, the Jews celebrate the feast of Purim, remembering that the Jews were saved from destruction in the days of the Persian Empire. **Even though the name of God is not mentioned in the book, you are very much aware of the providential care of God over His people.** God has, as told by many of the prophets, other plans for His people. These plans included, eventually, the blessing of all nations of the earth, and not just the Jews.

Ezra 7-10

As we saw in the reading of Ezra 1-6 and the book of Esther, only a small percentage of the people returned to Jerusalem even after being free to do so.

The things of Ezra 7-10 take place some 16 years after the people were saved from the destruction planned for them by Haman. **Artaxerxes** of Ezra 7:1 was the son of Ahasuerus and he is the fifth king on the Persian throne. **Persia** is in its declining years, thus the second world empire, that Daniel spoke about in Daniel 2, will pass from the scene, having accomplished what God had intended; the re-establishing of His people in Jerusalem with the laws laid down by Moses.

As we look to the time of Ezra going to Jerusalem, let's consider his importance. We did not do this for the first section of the book because Ezra himself was not a part of that scene. I think we can understand the importance of his being a priest, Ezra 7:5, but I wonder if we have recognized his importance as a scribe, verse 6. From our studies of the New Testament, the name scribe became an ugly word; and rightly so. However, this should not have been the case. In the changing of languages of the people, from the Hebrew, in which their laws were written, to the Aramaic or Chaldean, in which they spoke, there needed to be those who lend themselves to the intricate study of the law.

Ordinarily this would have been the job of the priests, as in the case of Ezra, but the priests were some of the most vulnerable. As far as the things of the world were concerned, they could not be depended upon to stick to God's laws and hold them up before the people. Thus, the practice became such that others, outside the priesthood, became astute scholars of the law, seeing that the position of interpreting the law was a very highly esteemed position. And herein lays the fallacy of the scribes of Jesus' day. **They had esteemed themselves higher than all others, in the knowledge of the things of the law. Therefore, they became more interested in the mere knowledge of the law and not the doing of it; a very legalistic view.** This is what we come up against in the New Testament.

But with Ezra both the priesthood and the position of the scribe are lifted out of the depths of human vanity. God had inspired Ezra to his task, **"For Ezra had prepared his heart to seek the Law of the Lord, and to do it, and to teach in Israel statutes and judgments,"** Ezra 7:10. Artaxerxes held him in high esteem, to accomplish his task, as we can see from the letter of authority he prepares for Ezra to take to Jerusalem with him, verses 12-26. Then Ezra says, **"And I was strengthened as the hand of the Lord my God was upon me,"** verse 28.

Those who were going to Jerusalem gathered together at an otherwise, unknown river called Ahava. Ezra had not asked for a military escort, because, as he said, "I was ashamed to require of the king a band of soldiers and horsemen to help us against the enemy in the way, because we had spoken unto the king saying, **"The hand of our God is upon all them for good that seek Him,"** Ezra 8:22. God does indeed look over them throughout the four month journey, verse 31; also Ezra 7:9.

Upon arriving in Jerusalem, Ezra finds that the people, along with the priests and Levites, have **inter-married** with idolatrous people as they had many times before. Read Ezra's reaction and prayer, Ezra 9:3-15. Many of the people, men, women and children, assembled themselves around Ezra and wept with him. Those who had married the idolatrous women vowed to put them away. Ezra made them swear that they would. **Then a proclamation was sent out that everyone who returned from the captivity was to gather in Jerusalem.** Those who refused to come would forfeit the ownership of any properties and also have their names removed from all registries, Ezra 10:8. Ezra tells them that they have transgressed God's law concerning marriage to women of other nations, verses 11-12. The men vow to put away these wives. Some are named who had taken these women.

Nehemiah

Nehemiah
Malachi

As we move into the final stage of the restoration, we can see how important men of varied abilities are to God's plans. Nehemiah could not have done what Ezra did, nor, as it appears, could Ezra get the walls at Jerusalem built. It was important to get the city fortified to allow the people to go about re-establishing the different aspects of their worship, pertaining to Jerusalem and the temple, without fear of the people around them.

Ezra said that it was in the seventh year of Artaxerxes that the king of Persia went up to Jerusalem, Ezra 7:7. Nehemiah says,

Nehemiah 2:1, that it is the twentieth year of Artaxerxes, king of Persia, he is serving the king as cupbearer, Nehemiah 1:11. **The cup-bearer was a very prominent and trustworthy position, a position which could very well hold in balance the life of the king.** The cup-bearer would often have to sip from the cup first, to make sure there was no poison in it.

We see, then, that the book of Nehemiah is a continuation of 12 o'clock, the Restoration. It has been 13 years since Ezra took that second expedition to Jerusalem. **Certain brethren had come from Jerusalem and told Nehemiah how desolate things still were in Jerusalem.** This makes Nehemiah very heart sick and he goes to God in prayer. He readily acknowledges that it was because of their own sins that Israel was in such a terribly humiliating position, Nehemiah 1:5-8, but he also asks God to remember that He had also promised the restoration of those who turned back to Him, verse 9.

The king notices the sad countenance of Nehemiah and asks what is troubling him. Nehemiah explains the condition of his people and the city of Jerusalem. Artaxerxes gives him permission to go to Jerusalem, with the necessary papers, to rebuild the walls, **"according to the good hand of my God upon me,"** Nehemiah 2:8. When Nehemiah arrived in Jerusalem, he went out, evidently in secret, to examine the walls, verses 12-15. He then goes to the people, verses 17-18, and the work on the walls was planned, certain sections to certain people, Nehemiah 3. **As long as the work seemed to be an insurmountable task, the people around them only scoffed.** However, when they could see that the Jews meant to get the walls built and to get the job done "in a day," Nehemiah 4:2, they began to pay attention. Nehemiah then had to arm the workmen with swords, shields and bows. Some worked while some kept watch. Some worked with trowel in one hand and a weapon in the other. They stayed on the walls night and day, only taking their clothes off long enough to wash them, verse 23. Therefore the walls were finished in fifty-two days, Nehemiah 6:15.

Nehemiah has the advantage of having Ezra still alive and teaching the law among the people. When Ezra went to Jerusalem, Zerubbabel and Jeshua the high priest had died. **When the walls were finished all the people gathered in one place and asked Ezra to bring the book of the law.** The people are willing to sit by the hour and listen to the scriptures being read and taught them. In Nehemiah 9 the readers go all the way back to the creation; and notice how each period passes before your eyes:

The creation, verse 6;

The call of Abraham and covenant made with him, verses 7-8;

The Egyptian bondage and crossing of the Red Sea, verses 9-11;

The journey to Mt. Sinai, verse 12;

The giving of the law and the building of the golden calf; also the manna from heaven, verses 13-18;

The wilderness wanderings, verses 19-21;

The conquest, verses 22-25;

The period of the judges, the kings and the captivities, verses 26-30;

And finally the restoration, verses 31-36.

Can't you just re-live all the periods as you read Nehemiah 9? Thus, the Bible itself recapitulates its whole story to us here in this last historical book. It never ceases to thrill me to read portions of the Bible that take me back over ground which has become so familiar to me.

When you can inject yourself back there in Jerusalem with these people, as they can see their temple before them and feel the security of the walls of their city around them and hear their scriptures being read in a way that they can understand them, you have caught the excitement I feel in the study of the Old Testament.

Then, after we go through the historical study of the Old Testament, we are ready to go back through, lay the historical view down and glean out from the pages all those fore-gleams of **the Savior of the world**. Remember how Jesus Himself began at Moses and all the prophets and explained all those things which concerned Him, to the two disciples on the way to the city of Emmaus after His crucifixion, Luke 24:25-27.

The study of the Old Testament will only **increase our faith in Jesus as the Son of God** and thereby increase our dependence on the Word of God as revealed to us in the New Testament.

May God bless you in your study of His Word.

FRANKIE LUPER

- STUDY NOTES -

- STUDY NOTES -

www.ingramcontent.com/pod-product-compliance
Lightning Source LLC
LaVergne TN
LVHW061311060426
835507LV00019B/2102